Love Like You've Never Been Hurt

Love
Like You've Never Been Hurt

Cari Jackson, Ph.D.

To order additional copies of this book, contact:
Xlibris Corporation
1-888-795-4274
www.Xlibris.com
Orders@Xlibris.com
126701

Contents

To all those whose
hearts have been wounded by
the ways family secrets keep the family in pain.

To all those who
believe that they are not good enough,
damaged, or not lucky in love.

And to those who
have experienced pain or violence in any form.

Acknowledgements

There is no coming to consciousness without pain.
—Carl Jung

Thanks to all of the individuals, couples and families, who through the years, have trusted me to sit with you in your anger, hurt, fear, and confusion. You trusted me to help you find your way to the other side of your pain. You are the inspiration for this book. As I have listened to your stories of heartache and hope, I have prayed for a way to help more people who are in situations like yours. Your courage to love is reflected on every page here.

Heart-felt thanks to my god-daughter Jenny Vallon who was the first person to urge me to write a book about relationships. Sincerest thanks to those who have reviewed and commented on the draft pages of this book—Derek Fordjour, LaChanze Fordjour, Selby Taylor Ewing, Tonia Paris Johnson, Dr. Linda Randall, Cynthia Wicker-Williams, and Dr. Robin L. Owens—and to Guramrit Khalsa, who proofread page after page. Your generous support has helped me to strengthen what this book offers. You have greatly aided me in saying what people's hearts have long needed to hear.

Deepest thanks to those who have both loved me and hurt me for you have pushed me to ask the questions that provide the framework for this book. You have been my teachers, my mirrors, and my angels guiding me into greater self-awareness. Because of you, I love more openly and honestly than I could have imagined.

Special thanks to those who have loved me and not hurt me for you have provided a constant safe space and refuge in which I could reflect on and understand what the hurts in my life were teaching me about me.

Sincerest thanks to those who I have hurt and have still loved me. As you have done so, you have challenged me to become a better person.

Eternal thanks to Spirit who gives me insights, equips me to frame what I see in ways that help people, and prompts me to write.

Never-ending thanks to Sheila, the love of my life, for being you.

Introduction

*The most intense conflicts, if overcome, leave behind a
sense of security and calm that is not easily disturbed. It
is just these intense conflicts . . . which are needed to
produce valuable and lasting results.*

—Carl Jung

Love Like You've Never Been Hurt is for people who have been hurt by
someone you love. If you've never experienced relationship pain, this book
will still be useful to you because chances are you are likely to be hurt in
the future. For we are all attempting to figure out how to love ourselves
and others.

For more than a decade, I've been a pastoral counselor with individuals,
couples, and families. But that work has only prepared me to some degree
to write this book. What has really helped me to write it is that I also have
experienced deep hurt in my own life. Nothing in the pages here is merely
theoretical. Every page is punctuated with insights that have healed me and
changed my life. And I believe that they can do the same for you.

The title of this book was whispered into my ear on 1/1/11 when I
was seething with anger and writhing in pain from a deep hurt brought on
by someone I cherish with my whole heart. In the midst of my anger and
hurt, I heard the words, "Love like you've never been hurt." My immediate
response was "No way! Why should I?" After a long silence—both me and
Spirit—I thought about one constant truth of my life: everything God
has directed me to do has always led me on a path of greater wholeness,
peace, joy, wisdom, and strength. So even though I wasn't clear about why
I should love as if I hadn't been hurt and even though I didn't want to do
it, I decided to give it a try. That is, I decided to trust Spirit in a deeper way
in the midst of my pain. So I told God, "I don't even know how to love like

that. All I know is how to protect myself when I'm hurt. I know how to run away. If you want me to love like this, you've got to show me how."

That was the beginning of a journey into deeper levels of love and trust for me. This journey has proven to heal parts of me that I didn't know needed healing, free parts of me that I didn't know were bound, and open me to greater capacities of love for myself, others, and God. It took hurting more than I imagined I could hurt to push me to trust God to guide me in every aspect of love.

Loving like you've never been hurt is one of those spiritual paradoxes. That is, when your emotional self says "Fight, flee, or freeze" to be safe and free from hurt, yet your spirit knows that going into the pain and transforming it is the only path to true safety and love. I have to admit, I have often asked Spirit why the path of these kinds of paradoxes often seems hard. I would prefer it to be different, but I've seen again and again that when I embrace these spiritual paradoxes instead of fighting against them, my life is always better, fuller, and freer.

Experiencing the hurts that I have aided me to see more clearly what my fears were. I didn't see these at first, because I was focused on the pain and on the person who brought the pain. As I went beneath the surface of the pain and the person, I got more clear about my own fears and hot buttons that were triggered by the other person's actions. Focusing on my fears rather than on my loved one's actions helped me to see myself more clearly, without judgment, than I'd ever seen me before. Without the hurt, I would not have known the ways that I needed to grow.

Let me share another admission with you. I am able to write this book not only because I have been hurt, but also because I too have hurt those I love. Acknowledging this truth has enabled me to understand all sides of the hurt that happens in love relationships of all kinds—between spouses, lovers, friends, parents and children.

It was never my intention to hurt those I love. And when I did, it was often a long while before I could really admit it. I could not allow myself to acknowledge when I was behaving badly or being hurtful because it didn't fit with my self-image. After all, people have always told me how loving and caring I am, and I am a minister and counselor. For years, I treated myself as if I were a one-dimensional person only capable of being loving, warm, and sensitive, and I assumed that I was incapable of expressing any other characteristics in my love relationships. While I could easily recognize the hurtful actions of others, it was considerably harder for me to recognize when my actions were hurtful because such actions from me were incompatible with the self-image that I clung onto as if for dear life. I didn't acknowledge how disrespectful, insulting, and down-right mean I could behave when I felt ignored, misunderstood, or abandoned, or when I feared that something or someone I valued was being taken away from me.

Once I acknowledged the ways that I have hurt those I love, I was able to explore why I had hurt them. Instead of focusing on the actions and motivations of others, I examined what was going on inside me. I began exploring beneath the surface of my rational justifications and intellectual reasonings to discover what anxieties and fears were influencing me—a loving person who ordinarily wouldn't hurt anyone—to hurt those I love most. It wasn't until I was honest about my capacity to hurt others that I began growing more deeply emotionally and spiritually, by leaps and bounds. Ultimately, this degree of self-honesty transformed my life.

At their core, relationships are spiritual opportunities to help you grow. By spirit, I mean, the vital essence of who you are and your unique expression of That which created you and all that is. And by spiritual, I mean, anything that influences or is related to how you express your vital essence.

Spiritually, the hurts that you experience are like the weight training you might do at the gym, the hills you might travel while running or biking, or the exams you take or papers you write in school. The process can be grueling, but is designed to help you to improve the areas where you are weak and build upon your strengths. As you learn more about you, the more you grow spiritually, emotionally, and relationally.

This book blends spiritual and psychological perspectives about relationships. Because so many questions arise when you've been hurt by a loved one, each chapter explores the common questions you may have. And each chapter gives you the tools to explore and answer these questions. Using the real-life anecdotes and reflection questions in each chapter will help you understand the dynamics in your relationships, heal those relationships, and most of all heal yourself. Love Like You've Never Been Hurt will give you more emotional and spiritual tools to love yourself and others more fully and freely. These tools lead to your greater peace and happiness.

So what does loving like you've never been hurt really mean? It means loving yourself and others with compassion, openness, and healthy boundaries that enable you to experience greater wholeness and deeper love. Loving like this is a process, a life journey in which you transform the hurts that you have experienced from stumbling blocks into stepping stones to assist along your path.

I trust that this book will help you as you take those steps. Thanks for allowing me to enter a journey with you into greater experiences of love. Blessings on your journey.

Dr. Cari Jackson
Bronx, New York
12/12/12

Chapter One

If You Love Me, Why Do You Hurt Me?

*You'd always say that you hate to see me hurt and
you hate to see me cry. So all of those times
that you hurt me, did you close your eyes?*

—Unknown

When we have been hurt by our loved ones, our minds race with question after question trying to make sense of what has happened and why. Almost always the first question we ask is: "If you love me, why do you hurt me?" We ask this question whether we are children who have been disappointed, rejected, or abused time after time by our parents or we are spouses whose hearts have been broken by the repeated disregard, disrespect, or betrayal by our partners. This question speaks to the core of our confusion and pain.

When you love someone, often you try to ignore it the first time he hurts you. You tell yourself that she was having a bad day, that she will grow out of it, or that she just doesn't understand how much that hurt you. You convince yourself that there must have been something that you did that triggered him to yell at you the way he did. You are certain that if you let her know how important it is for her to be there like she promised, things will be fine. You tell yourself that if you show him how much you love him, he won't hurt you like that again but instead will love you in all the ways you want to be loved. You convince yourself that the two of you can work through it and everything will be okay.

Just as the hurt is still healing, Wham! It happens again. Your parent, child, sibling, partner, spouse, or friend does it again. This time she even uses your words against you. She tells you that it's because of a hurt in your past that you are making such a big deal about this minor infraction. You try to tell yourself that maybe you should just get over it, and move on. And perhaps she is right some of the hurt you are feeling is from some old unhealed wounds. You try to begin the healing process again. After all, you don't want to stay angry at someone you love.

When you experience emotional injury it's like being rear-ended while driving your car. You are driving through the roadways of your life, and then all of a sudden, Bam! You are hurt. The seriousness or severity of your injury is not related to who was driving the car that banged into you. But perhaps, like many of my counseling clients, you tell yourself that because it was your parent or your spouse, your child or your friend who rear-ended you that you're not hurt that badly. Perhaps like many people I've counseled, you are not that comfortable being angry at someone you love. After all, they didn't intend to hurt you. You are right, they did not intend to hurt you but their actions did actually result in emotional, spiritual, financial, or perhaps physical harm to you.

Some emotional rear-endings are so intense that they result in you having what I call an "emotional concussion." An emotional concussion occurs when you are so shaken emotionally that all of your feelings are sloshing around inside you. The result is that you:

- are not able to think as sharply as usual,
- are more tired than usual and have changes in your sleep patterns—sleep more than usual or can't sleep,
- have changes in your eating patterns—no appetite or can't eat enough,
- have dreams that are more vivid than usual but seem to make no sense,
- cannot quite explain how you feel, and
- remember only bits and pieces of what actually happened.

With an emotional concussion, gradually things return to normal. As they do, you get more clarity about what happened and you become more able to reconnect with your feelings. Once you start coming out of the daze brought on by the emotional concussion and realize that you have been banged into, it is important that you seek help for you to heal. Get help from a friend, spiritual leader, a counselor, or someone else you trust to help you to focus on you. Someone to help you understand what happened, the impact of it on you, and how to begin healing.

I know that you're saying, "This is all well and good, Dr. Cari, but it still leaves me with the question of why I got rear-ended in the first place." The reason I've discussed your injury first is because as I address your question about why your loved one hurt you, I also want to encourage you not to minimize the pain you felt or still feel. Regardless of who they are or why they rear-ended you, you experienced love-hurt that needs to be healed.

So why does someone who loves you hurt you? There are two major reasons: unhealed emotional wounds from past hurts and uncontrolled anxiety when something valued appears to be threatened. Unhealed emotional wounds and uncontrolled anxiety are twins—two sides of the same coin that always work together.

Unhealed Emotional Wounds

Emotional wounds remain unhealed because they feel too overwhelming to deal with and are suppressed, they are minimized and their effects are unacknowledged, or because we simply don't know how to heal them. Our deepest unhealed emotional wounding caused by loved ones during our childhoods, parents and others we look to for love, affection, and protection is likely to go unhealed for years. As children, it is incongruent for us that someone who we love would hurt us. Because we don't have the emotional skills to know how to hold simultaneously these two experiences that seem so incompatible, we often suppress memories of our hurts or convince ourselves that "it didn't matter." And we often rationalize our loved ones' behaviors in ways that we make ourselves responsible for what they did.

The older and deeper this kind of unhealed pain is in your loved one, the greater the intensity is in how he will hurt you. Even if you never know what his emotional pain is or if he never acknowledges that he has any pain, his act of hurting you and others is a sign of his unhealed emotional wounds. The hurts inflicted by someone with unhealed emotional wounds are reflected in three distinct ways: knee-jerk reactions, projection of inner conflict, and normalized pain.

Knee-Jerk Reactions

Injuries that are suppressed, denied, or for which we blame ourselves can't be healed. Until we take the risk to acknowledge that any emotional wounding occurred and that it is affecting our lives, any of us is likely to act out in knee-jerk response. When the region of our emotional pain is tapped, even lightly, we are likely to say and do hurtful things without thinking, much like how a knee jerks up forcefully when it is lightly tapped by a mallet.

What can be confusing about knee-jerk reactions is that, at times, they can be presented by seemingly well-thought-out, rational explanations. When you dig beneath the surface of the rational presentation, statements made or actions taken in knee-jerk mode express thoughts and feelings that are inconsistent with what your loved one generally and genuinely believes about you, your relationship, or the circumstances.

I believe it was psychologist Carl Rogers who said, that in every moment we are every age we have ever been. When we have been hurt—whether during childhood, teen years or adulthood—and that pain has not been healed, each time we experience a new situation or person that feels similar to the original pain, it triggers a knee-jerk, self-protective response of fight, flight or freeze. This emotional reaction can come in relation to someone who either did no harm at all to us or whose harm did not warrant the intensity of our responses that came.

Think of it this way: all of you, at every age you've ever been, are all riding on a bus together traveling down the highways and roadways of life. As you travel, one of you, perhaps your 7-year-old-self sees or hears something or someone along the road that reminds you of a very painful experience. Your 7-year-old-self reacts immediately with the impulse to fight, flee or freeze, and tries to take all of you into the same emotional response. That's why sometimes you may have a strong emotional reaction to something or someone and not fully understand why. In those moments, you are experiencing an emotional reaction that is age-specific and situation-specific. That means, wherever you were developmentally at the specific age when you were hurt, the ways that you were able to process, interpret, and understand the experience are what guide your reaction to a current experience even though you may be 20, 30, or even 60 years older now. When you see very strong reactions in yourself or your loved one that don't quite make sense, that is an indicator that a younger self-within was emotionally triggered by something that is happening or perceived to be happening now. That is what prompts a knee-jerk reaction.

A knee-jerk reaction is a sign that someone feels attacked or threatened in some way. While we may not have conscious memory of some wounds, we jump in knee-jerk pain when the wounded area gets touched again, or if anyone simply comes near it. When we don't know why we jump and jerk, we assume it must be solely because of the person who was most emotionally close to us when we felt the pain. Often, this is the person we feel safest with to express what we are feeling. We project onto that person all of our emotional response that has been storing up for years about other circumstances and other people. We feel convinced that this person is uncaring toward us. And so, without really thinking, we strike back or run away as fast as we can.

Examples of this can readily be seen in very intimate relationships as well as in the random encounters of strangers. Here is an example of an interaction between strangers.

> Sam was on his way home from school one afternoon when Emilio accidently bumped into him. Emilio said, "My bad," and kept walking. Sam ran after Emilio and punched him very hard in his back, and said, "Who do you think you are?" When Sam was younger and smaller, boys in his school used to bump into him on purpose and knock him down. Even though that has not happened to him in years, every time someone bumps into him, it stirs up all the rage he felt as a young boy. His knee-jerk reaction had nothing to do with Emilio. [How the story proceeds from here has a lot to do with Emilio's personality, level of maturity, size relative to Sam, life experiences, and overall perspectives about life.] Unless Sam recognizes why he reacts the way he does when people bump into him, his knee-jerk reactions will continue not only with strangers but in other areas of his life. He will keep living on the defense.

Projection of Inner Conflict

When emotional wounding occurs during childhood, children do not have the life skills needed to process the pain in healthy ways. Because children are very self-referential and perceive everything in their lives as stemming from something they did or left undone, they are more likely to believe that somehow they are the cause of why someone hurts them, disappoints them, lies to them, etc., or that they somehow deserve the treatment they receive.

If this belief remains unexamined it also shapes the thinking in adults, in ways that are filled with inner wrestling and conflict. When someone hurts a loved one, in part, it is an unconscious emotional attempt to hurt the person who hurt him years ago before he gets hurt again. At the same time, it is also his attempt to resolve the pain by changing the outcome of the initial situation, but unfortunately often using methods that will not accomplish that intended goal.

At her spiritual core, she knows that she is not intended to stay unhealed. But emotionally, she blames herself for the pain she feels. When the spiritually-based knowing and the emotionally-based thinking are out of sync, she experiences an internal war that is often reflected externally. The internal war gets played out in her interactions with those who are closest to her. Sometimes, without understanding why, she will be mean and insulting to those she loves most.

Here is an example of knee-jerk reaction when unhealed wounds are touched.

> Throughout her childhood, Radha's father often told her that she would never amount to much and that she better hope that some man would show pity on her and take her off his hands. Radha knew that this was not true, but she kept wondering what was it about her that made her father say the things he did. She wanted to prove to her father that he was wrong. Strongly motivated by the desire to prove herself, Radha was very successful in school and became an attorney. A few years ago, she married Lalit who is also an attorney. Lalit greatly respects what a strong and capable woman Radha is. In their home, when Lalit offers to help simply because he loves her, Radha often snaps sharply at her husband and says, "I don't need you." While she usually apologizes later, the wounding to Lalit's male ego and to his heart is not undone by her apologies.
>
> Because Radha unconsciously still believes that what her father said about her was based on some perceivable weakness within her, she is still attempting to over-compensate or eliminate that weakness. Therefore, she is not able to receive and enjoy

expressions of love from her husband. Radha's self-sabotaging, knee-jerk reactions unintentionally say "I don't love you" to Lalit.

Reflection on Story. Radha's inner conflict gets played out in her relationship with Lalit such that she is very inconsistent in how she relates with him. At times, she is tender and loving and other times, brutal and harsh. While Lalit likely experienced some of those mood swings while they were dating and living separately, Radha's mood swings probably became more acute once they were married, leaving Lalit feeling that he was being duped and manipulated.

Like Lalit, perhaps you have experienced a loved one who appears to be Jekyll and Hyde. It feels very unsafe for you, as you never know which one will pop up. It may also leave you convinced that it is a well-thought-out manipulation by your loved one, "to reel you in," the idea of which hurts and angers you. Rarely are these kinds of swings planned manipulations. But because of your closeness with your loved one, you have been drawn into the outer expressions of an inner conflict, the magnitude of which you could not have imagined. The inner conflict becomes activated when a loved one's deepest wounds are exposed in the context of intimacy.

Normalized Pain

When emotional wounding happens regularly and from the same source, emotional pain in a person's life often becomes normalized. That is, nothing about the pain registers in his mind as distinctive or out of the norm. To the contrary, it is just part of the everyday fabric of his life. As a consequence, he might not even recognize that he is hurting. Because he does not realize that he is hurting, his knee-jerk reactions also become normalized. Others in the network of family or friends are often complicit in normalizing his knee-jerk tendencies. They excuse away his ill-tempered behavior, his "disappearing acts," or his refusal to open up by saying, "You know how he is." He is likely to regard your responses to his actions as hyper-sensitive and unwarranted, and say, "That's your issue, not mine." Instead of realizing that he has emotional wounding that needs to heal, he tries to convince you that you need to toughen up and move on. After all, that's what he did as a child.

So many of us are taught to ignore our hurts that they become woven into the fabric of how we perceive the world and our life experiences. Here is a story that illustrates the kind of impact that normalized pain can have in our lives.

Stanley's mom trained him and his siblings to discuss politics and world events every evening at the dinner table. As a single mother who was struggling to raise her four children, she wanted to make sure her kids accomplished more in life that she did. She was convinced that having a good education and being well-informed about politics and finance was the way to get ahead. Every evening at the dinner table, Stanley's mom would test the kids to see what they knew. Whoever performed best in making persuasive arguments got a special treat from mom that week. Whoever won got to spend a couple of one-on-one hours that week with mom. Stanley developed an aggressive competitiveness that helped him win most of the time. What Stanley learned at the dinner table has served him well in his work as a stock trader. While he won most of the dinner time competitions, he never developed loving relationships with his siblings. Actually, as adults, they avoid him because he makes everything into a competition.

Stanley has instituted the same dinner time competition with his children. While his son Gerard tries to participate in these dinner conversations, most of the time he just feels left out. Not even the prize of additional time with Stanley is appealing to him because his father never wants to go to the places Gerard likes. Gerard likes to go such places as museums and gardens; Stanley only to sports games and other places where people are yelling and competing.

Reflection on Story. While Stanley's mother nurtured a tremendous strengths of leadership, persuasion, and competition in Stanley, she injured him by not developing within him a sense of connection, compassion, and respect for other people's right to be who they are. As a result, he does not have intimate relationships with his three siblings, his son, and perhaps others, and he is not even aware of it. It is likely that when his wife, son, or siblings attempt to talk with him about it, he simply talks over them, drowning them out with his confidence that he knows everything.

Like Stanley, perhaps your loved one has normalized the adverse impact of the harm she experienced—something that made her less able really see herself.

Of course, some harms to children that become normalized are much more overt or severe than the harm to Stanley. Perhaps your loved one was abandoned by a parent and then minimized the pain of that experience in order to survive. Yet, because of that pain, he is less able to connect consistently in tender and loving ways. The tough exterior he felt he needed to develop as a child has become such a part of his fabric way of relating that he is convinced that you are the one with the unrealistic or too sensitive way of relating. Aggression is how he feels safe. Even though he is drawn to your tenderness, it also scares him and leaves him feeling anxious inside. It is scary both because it is unfamiliar and it stirs the tenderness within him. Being tender feels dangerous, even life-threatening because it seems weak. So the impulse becomes to do something to sabotage, stamp-out anything that might leave him feeling weak.

Knee-jerk reactions, projecting inner conflict, and normalized pain all work together in ways that can lead any of us to hurt those we love. All of these expressions of unhealed wounds are unconscious attempts to feel safe. The spiritual paradox is these unconscious attempts to feel safe always accomplish the opposite and leave us feeling more unsafe. And as a consequence we are more likely to increase our knee-jerk, aggressive, projecting behaviors that still don't provide the sense of safety that we seek, but instead leave us feeling more anxious.

Anxiety about Losing Attachments

The second major reason someone might hurt you is their anxiety about any perceived threat of their emotional anchors being jeopardized in any way.

Every human being has the same longing: to feel safe and to feel special. The extent to which we feel safe and special greatly impacts how we relate with others. Regardless of our age, personality, religion, family background, economic class, sexuality, race, education, or any other differences and classifications, all of us need to feel safe and special. While our differences in social identity may impact what things help us to feel special and safe, it is still the same emotional longing.

Safety is from Latin salvus, which means "healthy." It is also present in the word salvation (from Latin salvare, meaning to save, make safe), which means preservation or deliverance from destruction, difficulty, or evil.

With these meanings in mind, my definition of safe is: being protected from the adverse effects of danger, risk, or injury that impede health and wholeness. Being safe does not guarantee that there will be no danger, risk or injury in our lives, but that we will be safe from their adverse effects upon our total well-being.

I define special as being regarded with particular affection and admiration reflecting an individual's distinctive honor and respect among others. Feeling special also helps us to feel safe. Believing that if we are regarded as special, we have a guarantee that others will protect us because we are highly valuable to them. When we operate with scarcity thinking that there is not enough specialness to go around or either-or thinking that insists, "If you are special then I won't be special," our feelings of anxiety are greatly stirred. If we perceive that we're not special enough, the fear is that we won't be protected if the "chips fall."

I am the youngest child and only girl of four children. When I was about age 8, I was sitting on my mother's lap, when all of a sudden my brother who is five years older, knocked me off mother's lap. As I was landing on the floor, he positioned himself on her lap, the throne of her love. Ordinarily a 13-year-old boy would not likely seek to sit on his mother's lap, but my entrance into the family evoked a fear in him that he was displaced as the special one. My parents' plan had been that my brother was to be the last child. Imagine how much special attention had been given to him, the one who had been intended to be the last baby born into the family. My coming on the scene shifted some of the attention away from him to the newest baby and the only girl. His fear that he would not be special enough anymore overtook him and directed him to act out in hurtful ways toward me. He felt knocked out of his special place, so he knocked me off. His actions were the overt manifestation of what he was feeling inside. Even though his actions were directed toward me, they weren't really about me.

I share this story because perhaps at some time during your childhood you might have experienced something similar at home or school, in your neighborhood or religious instruction. Perhaps someone offended you in ways that left you feeling unsafe or less than special. Their actions toward you were in reaction to their own feelings of not being safe or special enough. For example, bullies—on the playground, at work, in church, at parties, or in politics—engage in bullying behavior because they think it makes them more special or safe to harass and attempt to control others.

When any of us fears that we are not being treated special or when we do not feel safe, we become more likely to have knee-jerk reactions that can hurt others (fight), create huge emotional distances to keep from being hurt (flight), or become emotionally shut-down and unable to connect (freeze).

Every human being has a set of things that we use as emotional anchors to feel safe and special. What anchors our sense of safety and specialness falls into six interlinking categories:

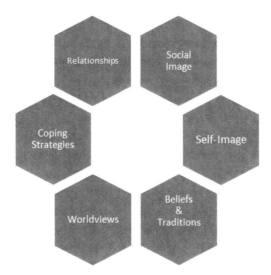

While each of these words may have specific meaning for each of us. Here are my definitions as I use these words throughout the book:

Social Image is a combination of your role (taken on or given to you in family or social relationships), reputation, social status, and material wealth that you present to the world in order to be perceived in a particular way.

Self-Image is how you perceive yourself reflecting a blend of what you have been taught by the words and actions of others about who you are, your interpretations of messages about you based on your life experiences, and your own inner sense of who you are.

Religious Beliefs & Family Traditions reflect a combination of beliefs, rituals, and traditions that have been handed down to you from your family and religion as well as those that you adopt for yourself. Because there is a kinesthetic (body movement) component to beliefs and traditions, as you practice them, they become an ingrained part of your being.

Worldview is your overall concept of the world that serves as the interpretive lens through which you see, hear, know, understand, and what you believe regarding your life experiences and learning (in German philosophy, die Weltanschauung). It both shapes and is shaped by your other anchors. It's like the operating system for your inner emotional-intellectual "computer."

Coping Strategies are emotional tools (prayer, drinking, domestic violence, work, religious zeal, sex, drug use, meditation, controlling others, high engagement with television and internet, denial, and so on) that you use to help you deal with life challenges and stresses that feel overwhelming. Many, if not most, of the strategies you use, you have learned from your family of origin, peers, and religion. Many healthy and unhealthy coping strategies appear in families across generations.

Relationships reflect the ways in which you are connected or involved with other people. They are the resources for learning about yourself and about human nature. They can be the resources for nurture and care as well as injury and pain. As such, they provide a sense of direction for your life, the kinds of people and circumstances to move toward or away from.

Our anchors help us to navigate the world. Without them, we would feel like ships at sea without a compass. The challenge about the things that help us feel safe is that we easily become attached to them. That is, we start believing unconsciously that if we do not have those things in our lives and have them in a certain way that we will not be safe and that life as we have known it will cease to exist. We believe that we will cease to exist. As a result, we feel anxious at the thought of not having our attachments. When this anxiety is high we will do whatever we deem necessary in the moment to maintain the object of our attachments. Most often we do this in very knee-jerk fashion without thinking or even realizing what we're doing.

The moment we become attached to these things in our own thinking, we transform them from resources that help us feel safe and special to the sources of our safety and our existence. In essence, they become our gods.

Often we do not recognize that we have made these anchors into our sources of safety and existence until we perceive that they are threatened. When our sources of safety are threatened, we feel threatened. As a result, we will fight anyone who seems to challenge or threaten our source, run away from any perceived threat as fast as we can, or become emotionally frozen and unable to communicate or make decisions.

Wounds and Attachments in Stress

Attachments to social image, self-image, traditions and beliefs, worldviews, coping mechanisms, and relationships, become more heightened in times of great transition or uncertainty, such as a new marriage or other relationship commitment, divorce, death, birth of a child, changes at work, financial stress, starting school, leaving a home that has lots of sentimental value, starting a new job/business, loss of a job, changes in our religious institutions, health crises, and so on. And these attachments become even more intertwined when we feel anxious and stressed.

These attachments show up in many ways in our lives—personally, socially, and organizationally.

- Siblings fight over and not speak to each other over who should get to own the deceased father's car.
- A husband hides money from his wife as they are going through divorce.
- Passive-aggressive behaviors show up as loved ones are determining what to do for the long-term care of mom who is on dialysis and has dementia.
- Members of a church, synagogue, temple, or mosque, who are generally kind, become hostile about suggested changes or how to use their finances.
- Business owners exploit employees to increase their profit during an economic recession, and justify that employees should be happy to have a job.
- Citizens engage in questionable political maneuvering to maintain socio-economic privileges they have enjoyed and block others out.
- Family members stop speaking to their sister and insist that she is lying when she tells about being sexually abused by her father.
- Parents kick their teenage son out of the house when he tells them that he is gay.
- A man beats his girlfriend when he doesn't get a promotion on his job.
- A mother starves her son who reminds her of the son's father who left her.

- A husband has unprotected sex with other women when his wife becomes more successful in her career.
- A young man shoots and kills innocent people when he feels like a failure.

These are just some ways that reflect the various hurtful things that people do when the fear of losing specific attachments—the things we transform into gods of our safety—intersects with our unhealed emotional wounds. The greater the attachments and the deeper the unhealed wounds, the more hurtful, and at times, the more heinous the self-protective actions. In the midst their fear and pain, people make knee-jerk decisions based on their fears not based on their love. Decisions and behaviors based in fear always hurt others, and ultimately they hurt the person who does the hurtful act. People who hurt others, especially who hurt their loved ones, do so because they feel hurt, hopeless, and helpless. Here is an example.

Daniel and Miriam met at work and have been dating for two years. Miriam has two teenage children from her previous marriage. Daniel is the best man Miriam has ever met, and she knows she wants to spend the rest of her life with him. She is surprised that she feels that way because she had been so unhappy in her marriage that she had decided not to get involved with anyone again. But then Daniel came and loved her so beautifully that Miriam felt safe enough to let go of her plan to stay single.

Because Miriam's kids are still upset about their parents' divorce, Miriam decided to not to introduce Daniel to her kids until she feels that they are ready. At first, Daniel was very sympathetic to Miriam's situation and decided to go along with this plan. For the most part, they only see each other at work. Now and then, Miriam and Daniel have dinner together at his place.

Daniel had not dated anyone in a long time. Several years ago, shortly before he and his long-time fiancée were finally about to get married, she was tragically killed in a car accident. Daniel felt that because he was slow and overly cautious about asking her to marry him, he missed out in having precious years with her as husband and wife. He had been slow in proposing marriage because he was waiting to have enough money for the kind of wedding and house in keeping with the lifestyle and social image that were important to him. Once he decided to date again, he promised himself that he would not make the same mistake of waiting to have everything "just right" before getting married.

Now, after two years of dating in secret Daniel is getting frustrated. Often when they have made plans to do something together, Miriam cancels because one of her kids asks to do something with her. She doesn't tell them she already had plans because she thinks they'd want to know with whom, and that would open a "can of worms" that she is not ready to deal with yet. Daniel feels like he's having an affair, even though he's not. Other women from work invite him out but he doesn't go because he wants to prove to Miriam how much he loves her and show that she is worth waiting for. Because he keeps turning them down for Miriam, his friend Josh told him, "People are starting to think you're a wimp. You need to man up and show her who's boss."

Lately, Daniel has been yelling at Miriam a lot. He's been saying things like, "You're gonna end up all alone, and see if your nasty children are there for you then. You won't have anyone to complain to either because you raised them to be selfish." Even though Miriam has been hurt by these comments, she understood that she has been asking way too much of Daniel and hasn't been fair to him. So finally she told her kids that she is seeing someone. Her children insisted that they didn't want to meet this man. But since they know, it has freed up a lot more time for Miriam to spend with Daniel. But as Daniel has said to Miriam, "It's a day late and a dollar short." The whole situation has triggered a memory Daniel has of always being the last kid picked for sports teams in his neighborhood. Every time, Miriam has chosen her kids over Daniel, he has felt like he's being picked last again. At first Daniel didn't remember this or associate it with his feelings about his situation with Miriam, but when he did and told Miriam, he thought she would stop picking him last all of the time. Since she has still been doing the same thing, Daniel began questioning how much Miriam really loves him.

Now, Daniel has become too busy to have lunch with Miriam. When they do have lunch together, he complains about her in one way or other—what she is wearing, what she is eating, what she does do and what she doesn't do. Recently, when his friend Josh asked why he was still putting up with Miriam not introducing him to her children, Daniel felt really stupid. Shortly after that, when it so happened that Josh was part of a team of staff making a decision about a promotion for Miriam, Daniel said to Josh that Miriam was a liar and was not to be trusted. As a result, she did not get the promotion. When Miriam learned about what Daniel did, she felt betrayed by him, and told him, "I'm glad I didn't let my kids meet you. You would have broken their hearts too." Although each of them had believed that they were the loves of each other's lives, because they were both so hurt, they ended their relationship.

Reflection on Story. Depending on your own life experiences, as you review this scenario, you might resonate more with Miriam or with Daniel as the one who was hurt. And depending on your own past or current hurts, you might see one or the other of them as the main problem. Actually, this scenario is about two people who hurt each other in different ways. Not because they didn't love each other, but because they both brought unhealed wounds from past injuries into their relationship and because they held tightly to the things that they were attached to for their safety. Miriam held to her children. Daniel held to his social image.

Miriam repeatedly hurt Daniel by treating him as a secret love affair, hidden away from her children. Because Miriam had been so unhappy in her marriage with her former husband, her only happiness had been her children. Unconsciously, she was scared to lose their love. She was afraid to trust that things would continue to work with her and Daniel. She was afraid that if Daniel left her and she had alienated her children, she would end up alone. She was happier with Daniel than she'd ever been, but still had not released the self-protectiveness she developed resulting from years of disrespect from her children's father. Her love for Daniel was great, but the grip of her pains and attachments was even stronger. She kept trying to inch her way into deeper connection with and trust in Daniel, but her unhealed wounds from her former marriage kept blocking the way. The combination of her attachments to her children along with her unhealed wounds from her marriage kept Miriam stuck in a pattern of behaviors that repeatedly hurt Daniel even though she loved him very much.

Because Daniel fell madly in love with Miriam the first day they met, he has been convinced that God brought them together. Since his former fiancée had waited a long time for him to be ready, he felt that perhaps this was his time to wait for the woman he loved. So he was waiting for Miriam to be ready and, at first, was complicit with Miriam in keeping in their relationship in the shadows. But because of his fear of the potential consequences of waiting too long to move toward marriage Daniel's anxiety was getting more and more stirred. His anxiety was also stirred when Miriam hit into his unhealed wound of being selected for the sports teams last. Daniel was so hurt that he began believing that Miriam was playing him for a fool. Believing this provoked Daniel to act very uncharacteristically in ways to hurt Miriam back. For Daniel, his reputation at work was very important to him. Hearing the kinds of things that his coworkers were beginning to say about him that he was "weak" and "needed to man up" hit into old wounds from his childhood of being perceived as weak and not good enough to play in the game.

At times, something that someone said at work or something that happened at home can trigger a fear in your loved one that one or more of her attachments is being threatened or attacked in some way. The anxiety that this can stir can lead her to knee-jerk self-protective reactions that are hurtful and attacking those who are closest. Your loved one can perceive that you are the culprit who is trying to take away the things that help her feel safe and special. The challenge is you might not even know what those attachments are. You might not know that something you or someone else did or said triggered her anxiety. This is especially true if your loved one doesn't talk openly and honestly about her present feelings or past hurts. Your loved one's pattern of choices in how she spends money, how she spends her time, what things she is willing to sacrifice, which relationship she makes a priority, and her need to be in control can give you important insights about your loved one's emotional attachments and fears.

I am not suggesting that because someone has deep emotional wounds from which he injures you that he should be excused and not held accountable for his behavior. Yes, people who have emotional wounds that they haven't worked through or healed are much more likely to pass their hurt onto others, but it never gives them the right or excuse to do so. To say, "love like you've never been hurt," does not mean to let people off the hook for their hurtful behavior. It does mean make your decisions how to love someone based on what helps you in your own spiritual journey, and what helps you to grow and heal your own emotional wounds instead of obsessing on your love one's actions or words.

Most of us downplay the level of stress we are likely to experience in times of change, especially when the change leads us toward something that we want, or when we hold onto a self-image that we can handle almost anything. If your loved was trained, like most of us, to tunnel through whatever life may throw your way, he might not realize how stressed and overwhelmed he is feeling. And when he doesn't, he is more likely to strike out at you and others who are most emotionally close to him. When he doesn't recognize how the uncertainty leaves him feeling unsafe, he is likely to blame you for why he does not feel safe and then to sabotage your relationship.

Each of us is responsible for our own actions. Each of us has the capacity to make the choice to acknowledge and heal from our wounds and the capacity to make the conscious choice not to hurt others because of our unhealed wounds. Yet, understanding why someone behaves in the ways that they do can greatly assist you in knowing that their hurtful actions are indicators of something going on inside them, and not a commentary about how much they love or value you. The way she hurts you is about her, and the way you respond to the hurt is about you. Your response reflects how you have been shaped by your relationships, your past hurts, your hopes, your attachments, and your fears. Understanding why someone who loves you would hurt you, is also an opportunity for you to understand why you respond to hurts the way you do.

Reflections Questions

1. Think of the people who have hurt you and the pattern of the things they have said or done. Also think of what you know about their past experiences. What do their hurtful actions toward you and what you know about their life experiences tell you might be their unhealed wounds?
2. What are the unhealed wounds in your life? Since some of them you might have suppressed or normalized, look at the patterns in how you respond when you feel ignored, disrespected, or abandoned to help you recognize your wounds.
   a. Strangers: when people bump into you; when workers don't give you attentive customer service; when you see parents being affectionate with their children.

b. Family Members and Friends: when there are money issues; when you are grieving the death of a loved one; when there is a serious illness in the family; when you and another relative keep being angry with one another and no one knows why.

c. Spouses and Partners: when nothing he does is good enough: when you are convinced that she does things just to upset you; when you want to tell everyone what he's done; when you rather spend time on the internet than with her; when you rather go to church or temple than be with him

3. Think about the person or people in your life who have hurt you. To which anchors—social image, relationships, self-image, traditions, religious beliefs, and worldviews—do you believe they are most attached, and why?

4. How have your loved ones behaved when they perceive that their attachments are being threatened?

5. When you are hurt by your loved one(s), what are the 2-3 anchors of safety or specialness do you rely on most to help you get through?

6. To what extent are you attached to these anchors? How do you behave if you feel that these anchors are threatened to be taken away from you?

Chapter Two

Why Do I Still Love You?

Knowing your own darkness is the best method
for dealing with the darknesses of other people.

—Carl Jung

Love can be very perplexing when you've been hurt. It's confusing to see something that once filled your heart with incredible joy become the source of indescribable pain. Your feelings are even more confused if your loved one has hurt you repeatedly. As you try to make sense of what you're experiencing, another critical question you ask yourself is: Why do I still love you? You ask this because part of you believes that it seems logical and sensible for you to stop loving someone who has hurt you.

Many of the great love songs that move us reflect the pain of still loving someone who has hurt you. Songwriter and singer Sade Adu captures the sentiment of this emotional wrestling in her song, "No Ordinary Love."

This is no ordinary love
No ordinary love
This is no ordinary love
No ordinary love

I keep crying
I keep trying for you
There's nothing like you and I baby

These lyrics reflect the grieving and heartache that come from loving someone who has hurt you despite your best efforts to support the relationship to live out its tremendous potential. Even in the midst of your pain, you recognize that this love is something special.

When you are hurting, part of you really wants to stop loving the one who hurt you. You may feel that he doesn't deserve your love. You may even feel silly and foolish for still loving him when he doesn't seem to care enough about your feelings. You may become even angrier at him when he says things like, "You know I love you. You know I didn't mean any harm." Along with your anger toward him, you feel angry at yourself for still caring, for still loving him.

Being hurt by a loved one is a much deeper hurt than an injury done by someone to whom you have not opened your heart. Hurt by a loved one feels like betrayal. So in that way it is a triple whammy of pain: the actual offense, the grieving that things are no longer the same, and the sense of betrayal. With the intensity of these feelings, you presume that you would stop caring, but you still do.

As long as your emotions are whirling around inside you, it is difficult to think clearly about what you really want to do and why. Additionally, while these feelings of deep hurt are gripping your heart, it is difficult to move forward in ways that are truly healthy for you. To help you get more clarity about your feelings of love and caring in the midst of your hurt and pain, let's explore three major factors that may contribute to your emotional wrestling:

- "Either-or" thinking about your emotional capacity,
- Your "love narrative," and
- Your human capacity for compassion.

Either-Or Thinking

We human beings are blessed and challenged with the capacity to feel more than one emotion at a time. Therefore, feelings of hurt do not cancel out love. That's why a woman who is in the midst of labor pains at childbirth can still feel love for the baby even as it feels like the baby is ripping her insides open. Or a father can feel extremely angry at his son for driving drunk and wrecking the car, while at the same time, feel tremendous love for his son and gratitude that he is alive. Or the wife who feels deeply angry at her husband for dying shortly before his retirement because there were so many more years she was looking forward to sharing with him.

I can imagine that you might be saying right now, "No, the pains someone experiences from childbirth and death of a beloved spouse are not the same as from a kid drinking and driving! The kid made a conscious choice that brought pain to his father, and the others were simply moving along with the rhythm of life. But consider this, when we focus on what we perceive to be the intentionality of others' actions, we are likely to overlook the unconscious motivations that direct their actions as well as our own. Our focus on what we perceive to be others' intentions greatly contributes to our confusion about our own feelings. When we perceive that someone acted with the intention of hurting us, we experience both the injury and the feeling of betrayal. Once betrayal is interwoven with other feelings of love, sadness, disappointment, grieving, etc., it becomes more challenging to understand and work through our feelings.

As we are able to look beyond what we perceive to be others' motivations and intentions, we can see the commonality in a baby being born, a teenager trying to grow into adulthood, or a loved one dying. In each of these scenarios, the common theme is progression, an unconscious effort to move out of what is known into the unknown, using processes that are also unknown. For some, this progression happens very smoothly; while for others, it is filled with gut-wrenching complications.

Most of us have been taught to understand our feelings and those of others from an "either/or" approach—that is, as either happy or sad, angry or peaceful, delightful or spiteful, distrusting or trusting, good or bad, conscious or unconscious, and so on. Because of this approach, we tend to lock ourselves and others into a box of feelings marked, "acceptable feelings for this situation," that often cannot adequately reflect all of the emotions that we may have in any given circumstance.

Much of the either-or thinking that frames our lives has been shaped directly or indirectly by teaching from our families and religions. For example, in my family we were taught, "If you don't have anything nice to say, don't say anything at all. As a consequence, some unpleasant, uncomfortable things that needed to be said were often left unsaid. And as a result, we did not learn how to speak difficult truths lovingly. Everyone was locked into our silence even as situations worsened.

Most religions teach "we have the truth, others don't," "express your spiritual self in the ways that we tell you and go to heaven, or otherwise you will go to hell," and "we are chosen and others are not." Through this kind of teaching, everything in life is framed as "good or evil," "right or wrong," and "love or hate." This either-or approach not only guides the lives of religious followers but permeates and shapes most aspects of human relations in many societies. A major consequence of this thinking is reflected in our tendency to see people as one dimensional and bestow either sainthood upon them for the good that they do or to villain-ize them for those things our religions regard as sinful.

The influence of the either-or approach is reflected in how we tend to see and classify people as all one thing or another—such as, the assessments we make about students only on the basis of a certain kind of book-smart intelligence and about those we regard as our heroes and sheroes whose wrongdoing we refuse to see. Because we have been trained to see people as one dimensional, we often overlook the dynamic complexities within each one of us.

So when we love someone, we unrealistically think that they will never hurt us and convince ourselves that we will never hurt them. After all, the fantasy thinking is "if you love someone, you never hurt them." The converse of this thinking is that "if you hurt someone it means that you don't love them." Neither of these stories we tell ourselves is true. The truth is that love is an incredible motivator not to hurt someone. But there are also other emotions that we can have simultaneously sitting right next to our feelings of love that might knee-jerk us to behave in ways that bring tremendous injury to other people, including those we love.

Because you may still feel the love from the person who hurt you, have the memories of loving times you have shared with her, or the longing you still have for what you want the relationship to be with her, you can feel your pain and still feel love. Either-Or thinking often locks you into narrow ways you see life and the options you can see for yourself. As a consequence, it greatly limits your happiness and your freedom. Here's what that looks like in this story.

Chao-xing and Françoise met at work five years ago and became best friends immediately. A couple of years ago, Françoise was promoted to head their department. Shortly after she was promoted, Françoise overheard some staff saying, "We know who's going to get all great assignments, don't we." Since then, Françoise often makes negative comments about Chao-xing when they are in staff meetings. When they are not at work, Françoise is generally the caring supportive friend that she had been before her promotion. Chao-xing has talked with Françoise several times about how hurt she feels by Françoise's disrespect at work, and has said that either this needs to stop or she will transfer out of the department. Chao-xing has tried to explore with Francoise why she feels the need to be insulting in front of the other staff, and said, "If you can't be my friend and my boss, choose which one is more important to you." Françoise kept saying that she didn't mean any harm, and that she was just joking around. But Chao-xing noticed how uncomfortable the other staff seemed to be when Françoise made her insulting remarks. Françoise has also insisted that Chao-xing was just being too sensitive because of how Chao-xing's older brother used to pick on her. At first, Chao-xing considered that maybe she was just being too sensitive, and tried not to get upset.

After several times of being embarrassed by Françoise in staff meetings, Chao-xing has told Françoise that to help them have the friendship they used to have she is going to get another job. Françoise assured Chao-xing that she appreciated her both as a friend and a colleague and promised that she would not make the kinds of comments that were hurtful to Chao-xing. For several months, Françoise honored her word. Then a couple of months ago, Françoise was back to her old tricks in a staff meeting. As a result, Chao-xing told Françoise that she was not sure she wanted to remain friends with Françoise. Today, Chao-xing handed in her resignation and told Françoise that was the end of their friendship too. Chao-xing was both one of the top performing employees and best friend Françoise has ever had.

Reflection on Story. In this story, Françoise did not know how to be both a friend and a manager. In her thinking, she could only be one or the other, but she did not want to choose. Because of her anxiety that she might show favoritism to Chao-xing which would undermine her effectiveness as a manager, she went to the other extreme and was disrespectful to Chao-xing as both an employee and a friend. Françoise wanted to prove to the other staff that her friendship with Chao-xing would not interfere with her role as department manager, but the disrespect that she showed accomplished the opposite. As a result of what they observed, her other staff did not trust or respect Françoise. Françoise was not honest with herself and Chao-xing about her either-or thinking and the anxiety within her. As a consequence she has lost two relationships that were important to her.

Either-or thinking can limit you from experiencing the depth and breadth of new possibilities for your life. And either-or thinking can lock you into relationships that don't work for you because it allows you to see only one aspect of what you get from the relationship. Most of all, an either-or approach to life can impede you from seeing all of who you are and seeing others in all of who they are. When you do not see yourself or others comprehensively, you are likely to experience hurts that feel like you are being blind-sided or undergoing a stealth attack.

Love that is framed by an either-or approach makes you more likely to see only the wonderful things about someone and overlook, ignore or deny the ways that they are wounded until you are hurt by their woundedness. And people's woundedness always shows up eventually. The more clearly you recognize it up front, the less you will feel betrayed when you are hurt. A both-and approach to relationships enables you to discern if someone is emotionally matched with you and what you seek for your life.

As you see yourself and others more multi-dimensionally, you can also see and embrace your multiple feelings. And as you recognize the multiple feelings you may experience when you've been hurt, you have greater ability to choose which feelings you will focus on and then make choices based on those feelings.

Love Narrative

The second reason you may feel confused and even angry at yourself for loving someone who has hurt you stems from your Love Narrative. A love narrative is an overarching belief about what love is and what you can expect from love in your life. Your love narrative has been shaped by a combination of your life experiences and messages that you have been taught about love by your family, friends, religion, and popular culture (books, music, television, movies, advertising). Your love narrative greatly influences the perceptions, interpretations, assumptions and expectations you have in relation to those you love, especially your most intimate relationships.

Here's an example with Angela and Yusef of what I mean by love narrative and its influence when you've been hurt.

Background on Angela. When Angela was five years old, her parents' relationship ended. Before her father José moved out, when he claimed to be taking her out for some father-daughter time, José would go hook up with one woman or another and make Angela wait in the car or take her to the woman's neighbor. As she grew up, Angela could tell that her mother Constance was still in love with her father. Constance was also convinced that no other man could love her like José and in her heart she was still waiting for him to come back. Angela's mother emotionally shut down so that she would not hurt again. Angela vowed to herself that she would not be like her mother: let a man disrespect her and she still love him. But when she got married, her first husband Tommy was a womanizer like her father. After Angela and Tommy's son TJ was born and things got even worse, Angela divorced Tommy. Angela is convinced, "All men are dogs. And if you have any self-respect, 'Do unto others as they will eventually do unto you.'"

Background on Yusef. When Yusef was still a young boy, he made a commitment to himself not to be like his father and older brothers who are very much like Angela's father. His brothers and father have always told him that he was "missing out" not having more than one woman. But because he saw how much his father hurt his mother and because of his respect for his mother, Yusef has always wanted to be with just one woman, be a good husband and father, and have a loving family. His mother always told him, "You're a good man." He wanted to make his mother proud him. For Yusef, "If you love someone you never hurt them." He also believed that "Mothers are faithful and will never leave you." Even though his mother loved him and was always there for him, Yusef's mother was not very affectionate.

Their Story Together. When Angela entered her relationship with Yusef, she often accused him of cheating on her if he arrived at home late. Angela cheated on Yusef at least two times that he knew of and said that was "payback." Yusef was not being unfaithful to Angela, so he thought that Angela was just saying that as an excuse for her own unfaithfulness. Even though he felt completely disrespected, Yusef resisted the temptation to hurt her back by evening the score and cheating on her. After a couple of years, when he thought everything was great with them and they were working toward buying their first house together, although she did not physically hook up with any one, Angela started "sexting" (sending text messages via phone that have explicitly sexual themes) with a couple of guys. She said that she's just playing around. When Yusef insisted that was disrespectful to him, Angela added further insults him and said, "Maybe I wouldn't have to do this if you gave me more of what I need." To avoid hitting Angela, Yusef walked out of the house.

Reflection on Story. Both Angela and Yusef brought their respective either/or thinking about love and their individual love narratives into their relationship together. And they brought their respective love-hurts into their relationship. They are the right ones to help each other to heal, but they got stuck in their pain and not knowing how to communicate with each other.

Angela had never told Yusef about all that happened with her when she was a little girl and the distrust of men that developed in her. She didn't tell him about because she didn't think was any big deal. Angela has a fairly okay relationship with her father now. She had convinced herself that it was all in the past. Angela assumed that she has moved on from the hurt she experienced as a little girl, but she has not. Part of why Angela was attracted to Yusef was because she could tell that he was a faithful guy, really committed to family. Yet because of her love narrative, she interpreted everything Yusef did as indicators that she should not trust him. Even though Yusef really gave her no reason to distrust him, Angela kept waiting for the "shoe to drop." Until Angela is ready to look at and consider perhaps that it does not apply in all cases, she will not be able to trust a man. The more she loves a man and the more she feels loved by him, the more likely she is unconsciously to sabotage the relationship in one way or other to protect herself from being hurt. Angela has a fear of abandonment and rejection, and a fear of being disrespected.

Understandably, when Angela was unfaithful to Yusef it felt like a slap in the face to him. He felt that if kept taking that kind of disrespect, he'd be a spineless fool. He was starting not to respect himself anymore. Yusef was angry at himself for still loving Angela. Why does Yusef still love Angela? He still loves how affectionate and passionate she is with him most of the time. Yusef has always longed for the kind of affectionate attention that Angela gives to him. He hasn't told her because he doesn't fully understand it himself. Additionally, he loves her because of how his own mother was always the one he could count on to love him and be there for him. When he met Angela and saw how she cared for her little boy TJ, Yusef felt safe with Angela and felt that she would never hurt him. Because family is so important to Yusef, he has stayed with Angela even though she has hurt him because he really loves her son TJ and wants to be a good father to him.

If Yusef and Angela are able figure out what is going on inside their own wounds and fears, perhaps they might find a way to rewrite their love narrative based on their love. You, too, have a love narrative that impacts how you show up in your relationships. Your love narrative may support you or sabotage you in having the kind of relationship you seek to have. Understanding what your love narrative is can help you begin to rewrite it in ways that strengthen your relationship. And as you look at your relationship as a whole, understanding why you still love, you can get more clarity about what works and what doesn't work for you and be able to establish healthy boundaries that support your wellbeing and wholeness.

A Heart of Compassion

At the core of our shared humanity is deep compassion. The word compassion is from a compound of two Latin words passire, meaning to suffer, and com, meaning with. It is compassion that stirs some of us to serve food on holidays to people who are homeless or homebound. It is compassion that inspires some of us to give money and time to help people who have experienced natural disasters to restore and repair their lives. It is also compassion that prompts people who have been pained by the tragedy of the murder of their loved ones to ask for life sentence for the murderers rather than the death penalty.

Because of the human capacity for compassion, when you have experienced love-hurt, a part of you knows that the person who hurt you is also in pain. Knowing this, even if you only know it unconsciously or spiritually, the heart of compassion within you cares that your love one is gripped by her pain. Your feelings of compassion toward someone who has hurt you is a reminder that no one controls or determines what you feel. You have the capacity to feel compassion and anger at the same time. You get to choose which of these will guide the choices you make in your relationships. Here's a story to illustrate this point.

JoAnn was riding home on the bus early one morning after working all night long. Just as she was about to fall asleep, a man and two children got on the bus. The children were so noisy and fighting with each other that they startled JoAnn awake. She hoped they would settle down, but they didn't. She turned several times and gave a glaring look at the man and at the children, but to no avail. JoAnn looked across the bus at Mary, who she sees on this bus most mornings to get affirmation for her anger. But Mary just looked at the kids and smiled.

Finally, when she couldn't take it anymore, JoAnn went to the man. As she stood in front of him for a long time, he didn't even look up at her. Frustrated and irritated, JoAnn spoke sharply to the man insisting that he quiet the kids down. He looked up at her, somewhat in a daze, and then explained, "I'm sorry, ma'am. My kids are a little out of sorts. Their mother, my wife, just died." Immediately, JoAnn's anger turned to compassion. She asked if there were anything she could do for him or the children. He told her no. Before she returned to her seat, JoAnn said, "I'll pray for you and your family." The children continued pushing and shoving each other and talking loudly. Their father continued to sit in a stupor. JoAnn felt so sorry for these children. She looked at Mary again, and Mary nodded affirming JoAnn's compassion.

Reflection on Story. While we often convince ourselves that we feel whatever we feel because of other people's actions that is not really the case. As we see with JoAnn in the story above, her feelings changed immediately when she got more information about why the children and the father were behaving in the irritating ways they were. Although the children did not stop their disruptive and inconsiderate behavior that was disturbing JoAnn's ability to sleep, she now related with what she was experiencing in a very different way. Adjusting her feelings was really about JoAnn's choice to perceive the situation differently. The change she made in her feelings was not based on the actions of the father or the children, but her perceptions. As a result, she shifted from thinking, "Those brats are getting on my nerves" to "Those poor babies."

Before getting the information about their mother's death, JoAnn had been convinced that if the kids stopped behaving in the ways that they did, she would be able to sleep. While that is highly likely to be true, the kids' behavior still did not control how JoAnn felt or how she expressed her feelings. Remember Mary who was also on the bus? Mary never expressed frustration at the kids. Instead, she was smiling. The very same behavior that JoAnn responded to with feelings of anger and frustration, Mary responded to with smiles and delight.

Often it is easier to make the kind of emotional shift that JoAnn made when the offense happens only once, lasts only a short time, the situation is one in which you feel you still have some control, or when the offense is done by strangers. Even though you have control over your own feelings and have the power to change them, it is much harder to shift your thoughts, perceptions, and emotions about an offending behavior when you have told the other person before that this specific action hurts you. It is hard to shift your feelings when you feel trapped in a hurtful situation. The hardest of all circumstances to stay in control of your own emotions is when you experience an offending action repeatedly by someone you love and you are in a relationship that you feel you cannot get out of easily or do not want to get out of. It is in these kinds of circumstances that you are more likely to give away your power to the other person and convince yourself that your loved one made you feel the way you do.

With common language like, "You make me happy," and "You make me so mad," most of us have been taught to give others power over what we feel. Truth is no one has the power to determine what you feel. Feelings are your human emotional responses to what you think about and how you perceive particular situations. While other people's actions can create the conditions in which you are more likely to feel certain ways, ultimately you determine what you feel based on what you think. Your feelings are your feelings. How you respond to what you feel are really your choices. That means, not only do you make a choice to feel a certain way, you also make the choice how you will express your feelings.

No one has the power to control what you feel. Your feelings are "an inside job" and are a combination of:

- your personality and temperament,
- your likes and dislikes,
- your perceptions about what you are experiencing,

- how you feel about individuals or situations from previous life experiences that seem similar to the current individual or situation, and
- the expectations you have about your relationship with the other person.

Together, these elements of your feelings influence how much you are able to connect with the innately human capacity for compassion. These elements along with your own self-awareness determine how you express your feelings that are evoked by the situation.

When you have already been offended or hurt, unintentionally you make your pain worse—more intense and prolonged—if you give control of your feelings to the person who hurt you. Allowing someone who has hurt you, to also determine what you feel, is like handing a knife to the person who has just stabbed you.

When your loved one has hurt you deeply, you still are moved by compassion. Within your spirit you know that the injury done to you was the knee-jerk reaction of your loved one's pain. Because you have the power to choose how you respond to your feelings, even in the midst of your pain, you have the choice to respond to the tug of compassion that pulls on your heartstrings. When you make a conscious choice about how to respond to the mix of feelings you may have—anger, hurt, compassion, hope—you can make loving choices that are also healthy for you.

Acknowledging your capacity for compassion rather than fighting against it helps you establish healthy boundaries. When you resist your innate tendency toward compassion you become more likely to build up bitterness in your own heart because you shut down the natural flow of love. When anger you have toward the person who hurt you is not also balanced by compassion, bitterness and resentment impede the flow of love. Fighting against compassion also leaves you more likely to flip-flop in your emotions and in how you relate with the person who hurt you. You send mixed signals to yourself and the person who hurt you, leading both of you in emotional circles and twisted knots. As you accept that the capacity for compassion is still within you even when you've been hurt, you are more able to make conscious choices about how you will express your compassion while you are healing. And the spiritual paradox of love is that extending compassion toward someone who has hurt you helps you to heal from the hurt.

You have the power, strengthened by Divine Spirit within you, to determine what you are going to think and how you will respond to your feelings that flow from your thoughts. It may be hard work at first to retrain your own thoughts and regain power over your feelings, but you can do it. As you do, you experience not only greater compassion for the person who hurt you but also for yourself. With greater self-compassion, you can feel a greater sense of wholeness.

There is no ordinary love. All love has the potential to transform the untransformable. Love has the capacity to reach into places within us that we did not know existed. The combination of the love narrative that you write, the extent to which you approach life on the either-or to both-and continuum, and whether you allow yourself to extend compassion greatly impacts your ability to stay connected with love. Instead of fighting against the impulse to love someone who has hurt you, seek to understand it. As you do, you will uncover important information about yourself and the person who hurt you. This information will guide you in how to heal your love-hurts, make choices that honor who you are, and foster your wholeness.

Reflection Questions

1. As you reflect on the stories in this chapter, whose actions and feelings most remind you of yourself, and why? What particular insights are stirring within you as you reflect on the actions and feelings you read about?
2. In what ways does either-or thinking limit you in your relationships? How does either-or thinking make it challenging for you to see things about people, including yourself, more clearly and fully?
3. Look at the patterns in the choices you have made regarding your relationships. What do these patterns indicate about your love narrative?
4. How does your love narrative help or hinder you in your relationships?
5. Write a new love narrative that empowers you to have the kinds of relationships you want and need.
6. Who are the people you tend to give power to control your feelings?
7. What helps you to connect with compassion?

Chapter Three

How Do I Avoid Being Vulnerable?

One of our greatest strengths is the capacity to be vulnerable. It takes great courage to be vulnerable, to open yourself up. That tender place of opening is at the core of our strongest emotions. Allowing yourself to be vulnerable is the seed for profound joy, deep fear, love, and countless other emotions.

—Cathy Brennan

Who wants to hurt? Not me! Most of us want to figure out a way to love and be loved and yet not be susceptible to pain. Makes sense to me. And yet, here's where the spiritual paradoxes come into play again. As noted in the quote from Cathy Brennan above, allowing ourselves to be vulnerable paves the pathway to joy.

Lots of us say that we want to be happy, have joy and peace in our lives. The questions each of us must ask ourselves are: "How much do I want it?" and "Am I willing to do whatever is necessary to get it?" All of the time, we talk about wanting to get a promotion, finish a degree, lose weight, become more physically fit, and so on. Industries abound that support us in achieving the things we say we want for our lives. And yet, most of us do not finish what we set out to do. Why is that? For three reasons.

First, our thinking. If we cannot imagine ourselves achieving or having what we want, we will not have it, no matter how much we long for it. Our thinking that things won't work out as planned blocks us from achieving what we want. Second, our attachments to the anchors (social image, self-image, love narratives, religion) or attachments to our unhealthy coping strategies (food, drugs, alcohol, violence, etc.) we already have in place to help us feel safe or special. If our fear of what life might be like without those attachments overwhelms us, we are likely to sabotage our own best efforts. Third, our comfort zones. Sometimes, it feels like too much work to make the changes needed to have the lives we say we want. We want it but don't want to work that hard for it. What all three of these reasons have in common is our fear of taking risks, especially if we're not sure things will work out after all of our risk-taking.

This fear of risk-taking shows up in very powerful and particular ways when it comes to love, knowing that there are no guarantees that we will not experience pain. So each of us must ask ourselves the question how much is love worth it?

The Risk of Love

It takes a lot of courage and risk-taking to allow yourself to be vulnerable with others. The word vulnerable comes from the Latin words vulnerare, which means "to wound" and habilitas, which means "capacity or quality of being able to do something; natural or acquired skill."

Typically, we think of vulnerability as being susceptible to being wounded or injured physically, emotionally, financially, spiritually or in some other way. But vulnerability is more than the passiveness of susceptibility. Emotional vulnerability reflects an intentional choice to use your individual human capacity to connect with others. It is a choice to make connection a greater priority than self-protection. This choice becomes clearer when you recognize that in order to know yourself fully requires you open yourself to intimate connection and vulnerability to others. It is based in an understanding that it is through our interactions with others that we learn more about ourselves—our passions, needs, joys, hopes, longing, and fears.

Making the choice to be vulnerable, despite your current or past hurts and fears, is an act of courage strengthened by your trust in Divine Spirit that you will be well. Each time you make this choice, you build your courage to take the risks of love, and your wisdom about which risks of love to take. And as you do, you become freer, stronger, and more whole than you imagined you could be. Vulnerability is one of those spiritual paradoxes—that as you open yourself to the possibility of being wounded you are healed. The paradox of vulnerability also offers that as you take the risk to move into your fear, you break out of that fear and any others you might not know that you have.

Cathy Brennan also says this about vulnerability—

> We cannot choose which emotions to feel and which to shut out. There is no switch that we flip that says yes love, no fear, we either feel the full spectrum or tone them all down. Less fear, less uncertainty . . . less love, less joy too.[1]

As Brennan suggests, your capacity to be vulnerable is your strength. Your capacity to open yourself and connect deeply with another human being is the seat of your truest asset as a human being because this capacity enables you to grow beyond where you are right now. Let's use the following scenario to examine what it is that we really fear about vulnerability to love.

> Jennifer and Tamara met at a party in the home of a mutual friend, Katie. Although they didn't get to talk alone too much that night, they both felt that they had to see each other again. The next evening they met for dinner and talked for six hours. Within a month, they told their friend Katie that they were in love with each other. As Jennifer put it, "I know this sounds cliché but I feel like I've known Tamara all my life." Tamara said, "I have found the love of my life." Katie was so happy for them, and said, "I know how you girls in love can be, so don't move in together too fast."
>
> Over the next several months, Jennifer and Tamara's relationship continued to grow more and more special. After a year of exclusive dating, they decided to move in together. After all, they explained, they were already spending most nights together as it was. Jennifer had the larger and nicer apartment so Tamara moved in with her. That's when things started to become rocky. Before Tamara moved in, from time to time, Jennifer noticed that sometimes when Tamara stayed over she got cranky for no apparent reason. Jennifer assumed that this was because Tamara didn't really have her own space in Jennifer's apartment. So when they were planning for Tamara to move in, Jennifer was very intentional about making sure Tamara took the lead on how they would set up their home together. Jennifer

willingly got rid of some of her favorite furniture to make room for Tamara's. They completely re-decorated the apartment to make sure it was their home.

All was going well for a few months—actually things were going wonderfully. Then Tamara started getting moody again and finding fault with almost everything Jennifer did. Jennifer tried to explore with Tamara what was going on. Each time, Tamara insisted that she was fine and then pointed out once again what Jennifer had done wrong. Jennifer felt like she was walking on eggshells in her own home. Instead of joyfully coming home from work in the evenings, she started staying at work later or meeting up with friends more often. And when Tamara found fault with her, Jennifer began yelling back at Tamara about her shortcomings.

Jennifer tried to make sense of Tamara's unexplainable mood swings. She wondered if Tamara had borderline personality disorder or if she were manic-depressive. Jennifer urged that they go to counseling. Tamara refused and said that they didn't need any stranger in their business. Jennifer has not told any of her friends what's been happening at home because she had told a few of them about Tamara's mood swings before they started living together and she fears that they will tell her she brought it on herself.

As Tamara's fault-finding about Jennifer increased, Jennifer began losing her temper more and more. In her frustration she started throwing things across the room. Then one day, Jennifer got real scared when she threw a book that flew near Tamara's head. Tamara also was scared and hurt, and she didn't understand how they got to that point.

Background on Tamara. Tamara's fear of vulnerability was triggered because the relationship with Jennifer was so amazing that she felt that she was losing her individuality. She felt herself "melting" into Jennifer's love and that really scared her. Living with Jennifer felt more like home than Tamara has ever experienced. In Tamara's childhood home, everything in her family revolved around her father Frank, always making sure things went the way he wanted. She was not accustomed to anyone putting her needs and wants first. It felt wonderful to be loved like that, and yet it was so unfamiliar that it also felt scary. When Jennifer went out of her way to show to Tamara how special she was to her, it triggered a deep fear of vulnerability in Tamara. In a knee-jerk response to her sense of vulnerability, unconsciously Tamara said hurtful things to Jennifer so that Jennifer would not have power over her and to push her away.

Also Tamara felt herself becoming dependent upon Jennifer's love, which left her feeling anxious. That anxiety felt like the anxiety she experienced when everyone in her family was walking on eggshells to make sure Frank got what he wanted. As a child, Tamara tried so hard to make sure that she pleased her father, or at least "didn't make him mad." But it seemed that nothing she ever did was good enough for him because he still complained and yelled. Without ever intending to do so, Tamara had become like her dad. The only thing Tamara knows about her father's childhood is that he was raised separately from his two brothers and one sister—raised by an aunt and uncle. She doesn't know why. She does believe that it left him feeling not good enough to be with the rest of his family. She does not yet recognize the ways that she is like her father; and initially would be pained, and ultimately liberated, to know this. Because the thought of talking with a counselor or therapist leaves Tamara feeling anxious that she will be judged, she does not allow herself to get much-needed help. If she has the courage to risk looking at this, she can allow herself to perceive her vulnerability as strength not weakness, and be able to embrace how special she is and how loved she is.

Background on Jennifer. Jennifer suppressed her hurt for a long while. As she did, resentment kept mounting and mounting inside her. For years before she met Tamara, Jennifer struggled with not feeling good enough. When she and Tamara first met, immediately Jennifer felt safe with her. She felt that she could just be herself in ways that she had never experienced before. In Jennifer's family, everyone talked loudly, interrupted each other, and insulted each other as a normal way of relating. None of that ever worked for Jennifer. Her older sisters called her weird. While her mom Janet tried her best to encourage Jennifer in being who she was, Janet could not really relate to her daughter, and did not understand why she liked to spend so much time reading, going for walks or bike-riding alone.

Jennifer loved how gentle Tamara usually was. That gentleness helped her to relax and just be. As a result, Jennifer was able to embrace more of her humor and even some of the loud and fast talking of her family. Because Jennifer felt so loved, she got great joy from doing things for Tamara, especially since she knew that Tamara did not get much of that attention as a child. She could not understand why Tamara would be so mean and hurtful to her when all she had done was to give love—love that Tamara expressed was just what she always wanted. When Tamara pointed out what Jennifer did wrong, it felt like the kind of verbal attacks Jennifer grew up getting from her sisters and it tapped into old feelings of low self-worth. Tamara's criticism took the rage that has been deep inside Jennifer since her childhood from low simmer to boiling point. She does not even know that this rage is there. After all, she loves her sisters. And because Jennifer is worried that others will think she made a mistake in moving too fast with Tamara, she is not reaching out to get fresh insights into her own behavior. If Jennifer can let go of feelings of guilt and shame for exploding the way she did with Tamara, and let go of either-or thinking about the feelings she has about her sisters, she can begin to heal the insecurity and release the anger and resentment that have been controlling her life for years.

Both Tamara and Jennifer were afraid to be hurt by love. They also shared a belief that they are not good enough. Their fear of vulnerability got in the way of them healing their low self-worth.

As in the case of Jennifer and Tamara, your relationships offer you the opportunity to heal old wounds. This healing can only occur as you allow yourself to be vulnerable—the spiritual paradox. Choosing to be vulnerable to deep intimacy with another person makes possible new opportunities to learn more about yourself: to see what your unhealed wounds are in order to heal them and what anchors you use to help you feel safe and special in order to have those things in your life but not be attached to or controlled by them.

Vulnerability: The Shadow Knows

As psychiatrist Carl Jung noted, each of us has a "shadow" side.[2] The shadow is that part of ourselves (our unconscious minds) that is comprised of our repressed ideas, weaknesses, desires, instincts, and shortcomings. Our shadow is not only what we keep others from learning about us, but we often hide it from ourselves. Running unencumbered within our shadow are the wildness, chaos, and undiscovered tendencies that are as much are part of us as our personalities that function outwardly everyday. When elements of our shadow appear in our dreams or visions, they make no sense to us because the behaviors we may see reflected in our dreams or visions are not consistent with what we would see ourselves do—that is, they don't fit our self-image. As we hold tenaciously to our self-image, when elements of our shadow present themselves in our human interactions, often we deny these aspects of our own psyches and instead regard them as exceptions, contend that someone else's actions drove us to aberrant, unusual behavior, or project these aspects of ourselves onto others. As comedian Flip Wilson's 1970s character Geraldine Jones used to say, "The devil made me do it!"

As shown in Jennifer and Tamara's relationship, when any of us denies our shadow sides or projects them onto others, we are likely to hurt our loved ones and not even recognize it. Also we can miss incredible opportunities for our own healing.

Our shadow sides can become intertwined with our fears about what other people might think about us as well. When this happens suppressed rage can come out even more strongly, as in the case with Jennifer, who grew up feeling judged and criticized when she was just being herself. Because she did not learn how to express her hurt and anger in healthy ways earlier in her life, when Jennifer did feel safe enough with Tamara, the conditions created a "perfect relationship storm" for her to express the full effect of years of anger and resentment.

Feeling loved and safe creates just the right conditions for us to heal old wounds. However, as in the case with Tamara, when feelings of love and safety are unfamiliar feelings, they can stir a level of anxiety in any of us that if unexamined or unacknowledged, will lead us to sabotage loving relationships. As with Tamara, our goal is not to hurt our loved ones but to eliminate our feelings of anxiety.

When both your conscious and your shadow sides interact with that of your loved ones, there are multiple tiers of interaction occurring simultaneously. There are tiers of feelings and motivations on the surface level along with other tiers of anxieties and ways of interacting that are unconscious to you and your loved ones. On each level there is an inner struggle that rages within each of you—a struggle between opening yourselves fully to the intimacies of love and self-protecting against the overwhelming fear of vulnerability. The extent to which the stirrings in your respective shadows are denied or projected, you and your loved one can become stuck in a loop of fearing vulnerability. Instead of your relationship being used as a condition of love and safety to heal old wounds, each of you clamors for a sense of safety and survival.

Signs of Vulnerability-Related Anxiety

To help you understand the fear of vulnerability present in yourself or in someone who hurt you, vulnerability researcher Brené Brown[3] offers six useful signs of vulnerability-related anxiety: foreboding joy, disappointment as a lifestyle, low-grade disconnection, perfectionism, extremism, and scarcity mentality. Here are my definitions of what these signs mean.

1. *Foreboding Joy.* This is the waiting-for-the-shoe-to-drop anxiety. Often, because of past hurts, he might find it difficult to relax in how wonderful things are. He can't relax in the love because of such beliefs as: he doesn't deserve it, good things never last, he will owe you if he accepts all of the love you give, or that he'll become weak if he relaxes in your love. Because of those beliefs, he is likely to start fights over small things or sabotage the relationship in other ways.

2. *Disappointment as a Lifestyle.* Because of so many times she has been disappointed before, especially by parents or partners, she expects that you will disappoint her also. She keeps interpreting everything that you do as a warning sign that you are about to disappoint her or abandon her. Not only are the things that you do indicators that you will disappoint her, but things that other people do are signs of how you will eventually break her heart. She may use some form of addictive behavior—drugs, alcohol, hoarding, etc.—to numb the anxiety of disappointment.

3. *Low Grade Disconnection.* While he may be the one who initially pursued you and the one who at times is the life of the party, he cannot maintain consistent social or one-to-one intimate connections. Short-term serial monogamy, adultery, Internet/ electronic connections, and hook-ups with prostitutes can be tremendous venues for the level of connections he feels safest in engaging, as these are more transactions than they are relationships. Transactions feel safer because they seem more controllable than relationships. The consistency, transparency, and inter-dependency that relationships offer and demand feel too overwhelming to maintain.

4. *Perfectionism.* Nothing that you do is good enough to her. You are constantly subjected to complaints about how you eat, drink, walk, talk, or even breathe. You are too fat or too thin. You are not

parenting right. You are not relating with your parents right. If you have abilities that she doesn't, she still insists upon telling you how to do what you do best. The complaints and competition reflect her own low self-concept that she is projecting onto you. As long as she does not feel good about herself, she cannot see you as good enough.

5. *Extremism.* Because he does not feel safe and at peace within himself, he bounces back and forth, up and down. You never know which of his personas (emotional masks) will walk in the door. He is very caring one day and extremely dismissive the next. He praises you and appreciates you one day and yells and curses at you the next day. This volatility gives him a sense of control because you are likely to walk on eggshells and stay in reaction mode to him in effort to survive.

6. *Scarcity Mentality.* She competes with your spouse, your kids, parents or friends, convinced there won't be enough love, attention, or specialness for her. When you start a new job or business venture, she discourages you or even sabotages it believing that it will take your attention or your money away from her. She is jealous of your success believing you took her share of the limited success that is available to go around. She doesn't show any interest in the things that you are passionate about because she fears there won't be enough room for her in your thoughts and in your life.

Everybody has anxiety about one thing or other. The intensity of anxiety varies by person by person. It also varies within a person depending upon the actual or perceived circumstances—based on how you at your different inner ages might be triggered. Anxiety in itself is neither good nor bad, it is just human. Having anxiety is not the issue; the real issue is how each of us responds to our own anxiety and to the anxiety of others.

Anxiety is like physical hunger or thirst. When your body is healthy, there is always a low-level of readiness for the body to eat or drink. When you do not attend to your hunger or thirst in timely and healthy ways, the hunger or thirst grow more demanding and can start to overtake your thoughts, moods, and actions. So it is with anxiety. It refuses to be ignored. Attempts to ignore it only make it more demanding. The most effective way to deal with anxiety is to investigate what it is attempting to tell you. It is signaling that something is triggering your feelings of not being safe or special enough. As you are able to understand what it is asking you to attend to, you can make healthy choices that promote your wholeness.

Sometimes you may not know that you are anxious about being too vulnerable. Any of us can develop rational explanations for our actions that hurt others. Such as, we're not really trying to hurt them; we're just pointing out something that they took the wrong way. Here is an example of how vulnerability-based anxiety can show up in a person who doesn't even know it.

> Cassaundra is the mother of grown sons, D'Andre and Little Mike. She raised her sons basically by herself after Little Mike's father left almost 25 years ago. Cassaundra was twenty when D'Andre was born, and twenty-two when Little Mike was born. D'Andre never knew his father. Little Mike's father Big Mike lived with Cassaundra and the boys until Little Mike was two years old. The main reason he left was because Cassaundra kept accusing him of cheating even though he wasn't. She started following him around believing that she was going to catch him doing something with another woman. No matter how much Big Mike pleaded with her to stop dragging the boys around on these stake-out missions, she kept doing it. Finally, he couldn't take it anymore and left. While he tried to stay in touch with both boys for a few years, having to deal with Cassaundra was more than he wanted to handle. So he gradually stopped contact with the boys. After that, she had a series of other short-term relationships with other men. But her two sons' fathers were the loves of her life. To manage her unhappiness, Cassaundra developed a drinking problem. Her sons don't remember the last time they saw their mother sober.
>
> Both D'Andre and Little Mike are married and have children of their own now. Because life felt so unsettled for them, getting married and really being there for their children is a big priority for both of them. The brothers are not very close because of the ways that Cassaundra always seemed to favor Little Mike. Even now, D'Andre is trying to win his mother's love, which gets on his wife's nerves. Cassaundra constantly finds fault with both of her sons' wives. Little Mike and D'Andre understand that their mother's relationships were a result of some things that happened before they were born, but they don't know what. They see that

Cassaundra has lots of contact with her brothers and sisters, yet in some ways they are not very close. For example, when Cassaundra is drunk, everyone in her family acts like they don't see it. Her sons did not recognize how secretive their mother's family is until they developed relationships with their wives' families and saw the difference.

Because they want to help their mother, D'Andre and Little Mike begin asking family members for some details that might help them help her. One main thing D'Andre asks for is any information they have about his father, thinking this might help. His mother has only told him that his father died. When he asks his grand-aunt Sally, she simply says, "Boy, you need to ask your mother. That's her business." After lots of attempts with Aunt Sally, she finally tells him that his father was the married man who used to own the neighborhood grocery store. She heard that he died a while back.

One day, D'Andre approaches his mother with the information he has recently learned about his father and asks for more details. Cassaundra begins to cry, and says, "Why didn't you leave it alone. The story I told you that your father died was a nicer story." After a long pause, she continued, "I thought he loved me. But I was just a young fool." In that moment, he understood not only why his mother had lied to him all of those years, but also why she had been obsessed with Big Mike, and why she stayed drunk. He does not understand why she seems to hate his wife, why she never got settled with another man, why she was always so angry at him, or why she was so emotionally distant toward him and his brother all of their lives.

Reflection on Story. When she became pregnant, Cassaundra's family supported her with food, clothing, and shelter for her and her son, but they did not provide the kind of emotional support she needed when she was hurting most. As she felt what she perceived to be their judgment, she was filled with shame. Her family's secrets about the circumstances of her pregnancy contributed to her staying locked in a prison of shame. Because she didn't have a safe space to process all of what she was feeling about her first love, when she met and fell in love with Big Mike, she lived with the anxiety that he too would disappoint her. When Big Mike did leave, it only confirmed what she believed all along, "All men are just after one thing.

And when they get it, they go." When he left, she also became convinced that something was wrong with her.

Cassaundra did what most of us do when we see a pattern of hurts in our lives. We presume that there is something innately broken in us. We presume that the pattern of our behaviors can't be healed or changed which leaves us feeling hopeless and helpless and filled with guilt, shame, and self-condemnation.

As well, Cassaundra, like many of us, also presumed that she got hurt because she had opened her heart too much, and vowed not to let herself be that vulnerable again. Because Cassaundra had not learned how to look for indicators of who was appropriate to be vulnerable with and when, she did what many of us do: she became self-protective and anxious. As the expression goes, she was a burnt child who dreads fire. But instead of developing a fear of vulnerability, we can learn how to be vulnerable in healthy ways.

What Will They Think?

Taking the risk of love involves vulnerability to a network of relationships. While you may be working to ensure that you do not leave yourself too open to potential love-hurt directly from a specific spouse or friend or parent, there is also the risk of having to deal with what other people think about your relationship choices. Sometimes that risk can feel even greater.

Being vulnerable to your relationship network can evoke your curiosity about what other people would think if they knew the full extent of the love and care you still have for the person hurt you and disrespected you. Or curiosity about what others think you should do. Or wondering how to honor what is right for you despite what others' opinions may be. How might you use your relationship network in ways that are supportive to you?

Sometimes you might intentionally seek the opinions of others to help you check the reasonableness of your thoughts and feelings. This can especially feel helpful when you are experiencing a mish-mash of feelings while you are dealing with an emotional concussion. Of course, who you ask is important. Because people who love you generally focus almost exclusively on helping you to avoid pain, they may not be able to help you to explore what the learning possibilities are present for you in the situation. They may not be able to help you recognize your own anxieties, unhealed wounds, and shadow side that are present in the situation or may have contributed to it. What they can offer, especially if they have journeyed with you through other love-hurt experiences, is a perspective of your relationship patterns and history.

Some family or friends in your life have responded to their own emotional pain by simply cutting people out of their lives or by denying that the pain ever happened. How your friends and family have responded to their own emotional pain will likely influence the kind of advice they give to you. To maximize the support of friends and family, ask them to focus not on what the other person said or did to you, and not on what they would do in such a situation, but to focus on you—how you have responded, what you have said, across the term of the relationship or across your life—relative to what you have said you want for your life.

Other people's perspective might help affirm the decision you're leaning toward or you have already made on the inside. Sometimes the decision might feel so scary—such as, stay in the relationship as is, stay but with significant changes and new boundaries, or get the person who hurt you completely out of your life—that it may feel helpful to have some emotional support. Again, if you invite someone to give you emotional support, be sure to have them focus on the goals you have for your life and have them help you assess in what ways your decision supports you in having the life you say you want.

Other times you're not really curious about what others think but have already convinced yourself that you know what their opinions are. So you don't seek their opinions because you believe that they will criticize you for the decisions you have made in the past or are considering now, especially if you acknowledge your love and caring for someone who has hurt you. In the story of Jennifer and Tamara at the beginning of this chapter, Jennifer did not seek out any conversations with her friends and Tamara refused to go to couple's counseling. Each of them, because of their fear of judgment and condemnation did not reach out to others when they really needed help. Similarly, Cassaundra did not seek help from others and instead drank.

So how do you decide whether to seek out emotional support, and from whom?

1. If you tend to rely on other people's opinions more than your own instincts and own inner voice, the opportunity for your growth is

to strengthen your trust in yourself more than on others. Before or instead of going to others go within your own heart and mind and assess for yourself what is right for you.

2. If you tend to keep everything to yourself because you don't trust others, your opportunity for growth and healing is to find one person that you share at least one piece of information with. Give them specific boundaries for what you want from them—just to listen, to give their opinion on one part of what you share, or whatever feels okay for you. Keep working to expand how much you share. It might feel safer to start with a professional counselor instead of a family member or friend. Start with someone who is not likely to condemn you but help you understand your feelings and explore your options.

3. When you do invite others to talk with about your relationship, make sure you select someone who has demonstrated that they can keep things private. Select someone who has relationships that are healthy or who at least acknowledges specific things that they have learned resulting from their own past love-hurts. Someone who is not learning from her own relationships is not likely to provide the best kind of support to you. Go to someone who is not likely going to tell you what to feel or do and impose what she would do, but instead focus on helping you discern what choices are right for you.

4. When you go to someone, ask them first to listen to all of what you have to share before he reaches any conclusions or tries to fix your life. Ask him to focus, not on what the other person said or did to you, but on what you need to do for you.

5. Use your conversation to help you practice being vulnerable in ways that help you to heal the wounds from the emotional hurt you have experienced and to develop healthy boundaries.

Reflection Questions

1. What are experiences in your life present or past leave you feeling most vulnerable? How do you tend to self-protect?

2. What are the most common indicators of your relationship anxiety—foreboding joy, disappointment as a lifestyle, low-grade

disconnection, perfectionism, extremism, and scarcity mentality? How do these patterns impact your relationships?

3. When you make decisions about your relationships, whose opinions matter most to you, and why? Does their advice leave enough room for you to identify and honor your own thoughts and feelings?

4. If you are hesitant to seek advice from a loved one or professional counselor, what is your greatest fear?

Chapter Four

What's Wrong with Me?

Mistakes are, after all, the foundations of truth, and if a man [or woman] does not know what a thing is, it is at least an increase in knowledge if he [or she] knows what it is not.

—Carl Jung

The 1970s song by The Main Ingredient tells us that "Everybody plays the fool sometime, there's no exception to the rule." These lyrics offer words of comfort to those who have been hurt in love and who are asking a common question, "Am I being a fool?" The song lyrics suggest that being a fool is inevitable when it comes to love.

Many of us believe that we ought to know how to love and not get hurt and ought to know who to pick as the object of our love who won't hurt us. When we experience love-hurt, especially more than once from the same person or in similar scenarios, we convince ourselves that something must be wrong with us for us to make those particular relationship choices. We tend to put very high expectations on ourselves and on others to know how to love and be loved perfectly. When we don't realize these expectations, we turn up the music for a parade of guilt, shame, and blame. We heap coals of self-judgment, criticism, and condemnation upon our heads.

Instead of beating up on yourself, consider this: simply look at the patterns of your relationship choices and seek to understand them—no criticism and condemnation. As you examine and understand your patterns of how you relate with those most close to you, you are better able to:

(1) Determine whether a healthy loving relationship is likely possible with those who hurt you, or if you are in denial,

(2) Forgive yourself for making the choices you've made, and

(3) Recognize the influence of your extended family system upon your relationship patterns.

Denial River

Denial is an important issue many of us wrestle with when we still love the person who hurt us and when we still believe in the potential of the relationship we've longed for. We want to be able to know if we are simply ignoring the facts or if there is good reason to trust someone again.

How do you know if you're in denial, or as some say, riding down D' Nile River? First, let's look at what denial is. Denial is a refusal to accept or acknowledge that painful life circumstances, feelings, or thoughts even exist.

You may use denial when you are overwhelmed by the idea of facing a particular issue, problem, or pain. Denial is a way of retaining a sense of sanity and the ability to function in your "normal" way in the midst of unbearable pain. It is a way to repress the truth by acting as if there are no issues to face. It offers a way to mask your feelings in public—if you don't let yourself know how much you're hurting, then you won't let other people know it either. This is especially important if one of your attachments is to your social image and you are driven by "looking good" to others. Denial is also a way to avoid facing the possible consequences of your situation, the decisions that you might be faced with if you acknowledge what your situation really is, and the risks of the change that might come in your life as a result of those decisions.

If you are someone like me who is accustomed to believing that you can or are supposed to handle anything, you might not let yourself know that you are feeling overwhelmed. If it hurts too much to know how much you hurt, you are more inclined to use denial to help you cope. The cues below will be really useful to you to ascertain whether you might be using denial as you coping strategy:

- Overly calm and relaxed in light of the circumstances
- Unemotional, apathetic, or indifferent in the face of loss
- Wanting to have a party or be more jovial than usual

- Caught up in fantasy thinking about what has just occurred
- Avoiding or withdrawing from people who want to confront the issue
- Increase in your unhealthy coping mechanisms, such as working longer hours, excessive unplanned spending, unprotected casual sex, hoarding
- Limited ability to give attention to your children, healthy eating, exercise, paying bills, household responsibilities, and other things you generally care about
- Less patient and finding fault with others about most things
- A heightened pattern of rationalization to explain away the issue
- A worsening of the situation as it is not being addressed

If you see these kinds of behaviors showing up in you, it is likely that you are using denial to cope with your pain. To assist you in releasing denial:

- Remind yourself that it is not a sign of your lack of value, worth, or strength for you to go through what you are experiencing. It is simply a sign of being human.
- Give yourself permission to express the full range of your emotions (including—feeling lost, confused, angry, or scared) as you confront the issue.
- Ask yourself what might be fueling your denial: "What am I afraid of?" "What is so painful that I don't want to face it?"
- Do a cost-benefit analysis: Ask yourself what the possible benefits and costs may be to denying the reality of the situation. Invite others to help.
- Risk letting go of the life you have known as you envision a new reality that includes the freedom, joy and power that you desire for your life.
- Remind yourself that you can use the painful experience of the issue/problem to heal, learn and grow in ways that help you live more fully as the person you desire to be.

Also, here are few questions to ask yourself that may help: (1) What indicators are there that she acknowledges that her actions hurt you, and how? (2) Is he more focused on defending himself and what he did than on expressing genuine empathy and caring for you? (3) What indicators there are that she has the courage to look at her own issues and explore what triggered her to behave in ways that were hurtful to you? (4) To what extent does he demonstrate a willingness to make amends and make changes in how he relates with you?

Doing this self-reflection can help you discern whether you are in denial, and if so, how to break free from it. Once you have more clarity about the impact of your love-hurt and how you are coping with it, you are better able to assess the relationship with the person who hurt you, whether or not there are sufficient healthy reasons for you to continue the relationship, and if so, what new healthy boundaries you may choose to put in place. Also see Chapter 8 "Why, Who, and How to Trust Again?" for more tools to help you get clearer about how you want to move forward and not feel like a fool for loving.

Self-Forgiveness

The opening quote for this chapter from Jung reminds us that we do make mistakes—that is, make choices that take us away from where we are attempting to go, what we are seeking to accomplish, or who we are longing to be in our lives. It is human to do so. Mistakes, as Jung says, "are the foundations of truth." It is through our reflection on our mistakes that we learn. But understand, mistakes only give us the opportunity to learn. In order to use mistakes as the foundations of truth and learning, we must forgive ourselves.

As reflected in the story of Cassaundra, she spent thirty or more years, seeing herself as a fool for loving and getting pregnant by a man who she later learned wanted her only for sex. Because she never forgave herself, the only beliefs she came away from the experience with were: "men only want one thing" and "something's wrong with me." She did not discover the truth about her incredible capacity to love. That truth remained hidden from her, her sons, and extended family throughout the years. Even now, if Cassaundra could understand more why she made the choices that she made, she could forgive herself and get to her truth by understanding the generational pains that set the stage for her pains. Let me share more about Cassaundra's story.

Cassaundra was the fifth of nine children. All nine were born within twelve years. All of her childhood, Cassaundra's mother Betty was depressed and her father Max was drunk. The family lived in a three-bedroom house. There was no privacy, no quiet space in the house. As a child, Cassaundra loved to draw, paint, and make things from clay or whatever she could get her hands on. But in her family there was no time, money, or appreciation for art.

Boys were always telling Cassaundra how beautiful she was and were often trying to get her to have sex with them. Her mother never talked with her about sex or birth control other than, "Keep your legs shut." But she was clear that she wanted much more for her life than having babies. She wanted to get out of the neighborhood she grew up in and see the world. She wanted to be an artist in New York or Paris or Rome. When she said this to her family, they shook their heads at her, and said, "Oh, we not good enough for you?"

Because money was tight, everyone was expected to start working as kids. Cassaundra had a series of little odd jobs such as, raking, cleaning, and running errands for people starting at age six. When she was sixteen, she landed a job working at the neighborhood grocery store. She had known the owner, Mr. Greenbaum since she was a little girl. He was the only one who took an interest in her goals to be an artist and travel the world. Once he took her to an art museum, and she fell in love with him. When Mr. Greenbaum helped Cassaundra get a full scholarship to art school, she was convinced that he was in love with her too. Periodically he would say to her, "You're getting so beautiful, I'm gonna have to leave my wife for you one day." When Mr. Greenbaum asked her to have sex with him, she said no, but eventually she agreed. She became pregnant. When she told Mr. Greenbaum, he told her that he would take her to "fix this situation." Because of her love for Mr. Greenbaum, Cassaundra wanted to keep the baby and thought that he would be happy. But instead, he fired her from her job and told her never to step foot in the store again or he would have her arrested. Cassaundra became depressed, dropped out of art school and endured the gloating she received from her family. In their minds, now she was down to their level. She never returned to art or left the neighborhood.

Cassaundra could not forgive herself because she felt so stupid to have "been played" by Mr. Greenbaum, whose first name she never knew. Her dreams were all crushed in a moment. She felt that she should have seen it that he was after that same thing as all the rest of the boys in her neighborhood. She was close to graduating from art school but was too depressed to finish.

Reflection on Story. Cassaundra has not factored in how much of her choices with Mr. Greenbaum and later with Big Mike were shaped by the truth that she was simply looking for love. She didn't realize that even though she was 20 years old, Mr. Greenbaum knew a lot more than she did. Even though her family took care of her through her depression and pregnancy and helped her when her baby came, she did not feel emotionally supported by them. As soon as she could she moved out, but she brought her sense of her family's condemnation with her. Not feeling loved by her family, when she met Big Mike and felt loved by him, she became so anxious that he would leave that her smothering actions became a self-fulfilling prophecy and prompted him to leave. She never let herself open up her heart to another man after that, not even to her sons. For Cassaundra, D'Andre was a constant reminder to her of what a fool she was and that something was wrong with her.

I remember when my mother was dealing with a situation that she had never dealt with before. When she discovered the mistake she made, she was beating up on herself, saying, "I should have known better." I pointed out to her that she had never dealt with anything like it before and asked her why she should have known better. She responded, "Because I'm 75!"

Whether 20 like Cassaundra or 75 like my mother, we don't magically know things because of our age. It is experience that teaches us. We learn when the lesson presents itself. Perhaps you have made mistakes or choices in your life that you think, "I should have known better." Well, you are not all-knowing and all-wise. Forgive yourself. Learn from the situation. And allow it to become the foundation of your truth. Remind yourself, "There's nothing wrong with me, I am a learner."

As you learn, there will be some emotional lessons that may take you longer and more repeated experiences for you to learn than it may someone else. That's okay. Everybody is slower in learning one thing or other. That means, for each of us, there is one emotional issue or another that it seems take a long time for us to learn the truth of. Because of your particular early experiences and how you have been socialized to think about your mistakes, and what your particular spiritual lessons and spiritual purpose may be, what you need to learn and how long it takes you is about your spiritual journey. No need to compare yourself with anyone else. Comparing yourself with others actually slows down your learning because it distract you from your journey and saps your energy as you shame yourself about one thing or other. Just learn what there is for you to learn. As you learn you can forgive. It is the path to your wholeness.

So how do you forgive yourself? The answer to this may vary person to person and situation to situation, but here are a few strategies that might be useful to you.

1. *Remember you can only do what you know how to do.* Life really is an ongoing learning experience. Just as in school, if you have not learned algebra, even if you're great at doing geometry, when you are presented with an algebraic equation, it is not likely that you will solve the equation easily. That doesn't mean that you're not smart, or that anything is wrong with you. You simply do not know how to do it. Throughout your life, you will come across situations in your relationships that you simply do not know how to handle. Ask for guidance from angels, ancestors, trusted loved ones, spiritual leaders, or counselors to help you learn. Be gracious and gentle to yourself as you are learning. The more gentle and kind you are to yourself, the faster you will learn. Conversely, being angry at yourself slows your learning process.

2. *Love the little child within you.* Remember that in every moment you are every age you have ever been. When you have made choices in love that have not seemed to turn out well, the little child within you feels very guilty and ashamed. Guilt and shame are not the conditions for healing and growth. Your little-child-within needs to feel safe in order for learn, grow, and flourish. Your little-child-within needs and deserves your compassion and caring no matter what.

3. *Speak affirming words to yourself about yourself.* When you've made choices that have invited pain into your life, either because you hurt someone you love or you were the one who was hurt, you might be inclined speak words that belittle you and beat up on you. Even if you feel that you deserve those words, such words never create the

conditions for you to learn from your mistakes. Instead, speaking words of defeat leave you more likely to live defeated. You do not learn your best or thrive under duress. Instead, speak words that acknowledge the situation and that affirm what you intend to learn from the situation—such as, "I didn't get it right this time, but I will" or "I didn't stay in the mess as long as I did last time."

4. *Remember that your actions were knee-jerk reactions to your pain, anxiety and fear.* When you are in a knee-jerk mode, you do not think as clearly as you might ordinarily do. The choices you make when you are in pain, anxious, or scared are not likely to be your best. Accept that reality, even as you may have real consequences that you must deal with as a result of your actions. Understand what you were reacting to, and identify if there are changes you can make either in your perceptions or in the situation. As you do, in order to avoid making the situation worse, make any needed changes guided by love, not fear.

5. *Shift your focus from what you've done to what is now possible.* Remember, that it's not over, 'til it's over. The choice you made, even with all of the challenges and consequences that come with it, might be the very thing needed in your life to usher you into the new place you need to be for your healing, learning, and growing. If you understand that your choice, even with the harm and pain it brought to you and others, is not the end of your story. Instead it can be used as a key element to move your story forward. Instead of your life story being about someone who always gets everything perfectly right, perhaps your story is about someone who is an overcomer. Regardless of what you've written in your life story so far, now you have new opportunities that weren't possible until the choice you made. You were unconsciously setting yourself up for something better.

6. *Know that you are more than your mistakes.* Who you are and what your potential is are greater than the choices you have made. Sometimes it might be difficult for you to forgive yourself because you're disappointed with yourself. When you have a particular self-image and the choices you made don't fit with how you see yourself, you are likely to believe that your choices define you. As you wrestle against this new unacceptable definition of you, you stay stuck in a fight of you against you. Yes, understand that your actions are giving you important information about you, but they

do not define you. It is how you respond to the mistakes you've made that define you. Think about people like Mohandas Gandhi, who did not excel academically or professionally and still became a great political leader who changed the course of history in his homeland and around the world. You are more than your shortcomings, your crazy choices and your repeated mistakes. There is greatness inside you.

7. *Ask for guidance from Spirit to help you to forgive yourself.* Sometimes you may be so disappointed with yourself that you feel that you don't deserve to be forgiven. That's when support from God, angels, and ancestors can be very helpful. Divine Spirit can help you to know that you have already been forgiven by That which made you. Divine Spirit, looks beyond the mistakes, the poor choices you've made, knowing that there are incredible opportunities for learning and healing that come as a result of those missteps. Instead of seeing those missteps as if they tell the entire story as a movie of your life, Spirit knows that those steps are only still frames of your life.

Generational Coping Strategies

What we learn directly and indirectly from our family systems—both immediate family members and generations of extended family—plays a tremendous role in how we cope with love-hurts and other life challenges. Families pass from one generation to the next patterns of how to deal with emotional pain, anxiety, and stress. As a consequence, families develop and pass on both healthy and unhealthy coping strategies, such as drinking, prayer, secrecy, denial, dancing, domestic violence, eating, working, incest, acting as if nothing happened, and so on. The coping strategies that we learn in our family systems greatly influence how we see ourselves, the choices we believe we have in our relationships, and the degree of resiliency we have when we've been hurt.

To illustrate this point, let's look at the family dynamics in Cassaundra's family to understand what contributed to Cassaundra's choices: relating to male partners, her belief that she was unlucky in love, her relationship with her sons, her choice to use alcohol to numb her pain, and her inability to follow her plans to pursue her dreams once she became pregnant.

Since her childhood, Cassaundra had always felt like the odd person out. Every time her siblings made fun of her, her mother was silent and her father told her "that's a stupid idea, Miss High and Mighty."

What none of the kids knew was that their father Max had been an artist as well. Similar to his daughter, Max had dreamed of living in New York City to paint and sculpt. His mother died when he was four years old, and that same day his father suddenly disappeared. Max's father's sister, Sally, raised him but she never told him how his mother died or why his father left. Because there weren't many opportunities available for him to pursue his dream, Max enlisted in the army at age 15 so that he could see the world. Once he experienced the harsh realities of war, he never painted again. When he returned to his home city, he started drinking in an attempt to wipe visions of death and destruction that haunted him. Shortly after he returned, he met Betty and they had their first child together. Max was not in love with Betty but since he had no family, he decided to get married. As each child came, he worked harder and drank harder as his way of dealing with feeling more and more trapped in his life.

Cassaundra's mother Betty knew that Max didn't love her but she was glad that he was committed to his family. Betty grew up in the foster care system. Until about age three, she lived with her mother. She was taken from her mother because of child abuse and neglect. Betty never learned that she was a child of rape. As a young girl, she decided that she wanted to have a big family and she wanted to become a social worker to help children. Once she got pregnant and started having children, Betty gave up on her professional dreams and instead focused on having babies. Her children were her only joy in her life. She felt that if she didn't have her babies, she wouldn't have anyone to love her. While she loved her kids, she did not know how to be tender and gentle with them because she had never experienced that herself. As her children became older and didn't need her as much, she became more depressed.

Reflection on Generational Impact. Cassaundra's story is really about at least five generations: her parents' parents, her parents, herself and her siblings, her sons and, and her grandchildren and all of the in-laws and cousins in each generation.

Neither Betty nor Max learned how to talk about their feelings. They remained silent in their pains. Both of them had given up on their dreams and as a result felt angry, sad, and emotionally empty. By the time Cassaundra was born, everyone in the family knew to be silent about any dreams they had and just settle with what you get. The silences then became secrets.

Cassaundra had no idea that she was repeating choices that each of her parents had made. Choices based on believing that she had limited options available for her life. It was ingrained in her from her father that her vision of becoming a great artist was a stupid idea. She was convinced that something was wrong with her for wanting the things she did. When things did not work out as she planned, she figured that she was destined to stay in the in the little house and be a nobody. In part because she felt how unhappy her mother was in love, Cassaundra assumed that it was her fate to be unlucky in love like her mother and her sisters.

Cassaundra's family members were silent about the circumstances of her pregnancy for decades. The secrecy was not distinctive to her relationship with Mr. Greenbaum. Secrecy and denial were coping strategies used in her family for generations. As a result of family systems of secrecy, Max didn't know the circumstances surrounding his mother's death and Betty didn't know the circumstances of her birth. When these two people who did not know how to talk about the pains from love-hurts and life disappointment raised their children, they instilled in them the only ways they knew how to deal with love-hurts: silence, secretiveness, denial, attaching to your kids to fill your emotional void, sex, drinking, working hard and emotionally shutting down.

Because of the secrets, Cassaundra never felt good enough and felt that something was wrong with her. She did not get any emotional support from her family when she realized that the man she loved was only using her because her parents did not know how to give the kind of support she needed. Both of her parents were adamant about "accepting the hand that life deals you." Max could not encourage his daughter to pursue her dreams because he did not want her to get hurt like he did. Betty couldn't understand Cassaundra's pain, because from her perspective her daughter should have been satisfied that she got a baby to love her.

Guided by her love narrative that "men only want to use you, and when you give into them, they leave," Cassaundra's relationships with males were limited in two ways. First, although she had many male partners, she could not relax enough in the relationships to trust them and really be emotionally intimate with them. Second, she was unable to develop a real closeness with her sons because she convinced that they would grow up and hurt her just like all of the other men in her life. Even now, despite all that they do to show their love and to win her love, Cassaundra became even more convinced that her boys would abandon her when they started their own families. For that reason she doesn't like their wives and her relationship with her grandchildren flips back and forth from frequent contact to virtually none at all. Because of her emotional wounding there's not enough that her sons can do to satisfy her.

Future Generations. Both Little Mike and D'Andre see effects of their mother's patterns showing up in their relationships. This is especially true for D'Andre. Growing up seeing how his mother was more loving toward his brother, D'Andre always felt that he was not good enough. He has spent much of his life trying to be good enough to deserve his mother's love. He competes with his brother in trying to do more for their mother. So while he and his brother love each other, there is also a tension in their relationship. In his marriage, D'Andre has challenges being consistently emotionally intimate with his wife even though he loves her very much. Sometimes he focuses more on his mother than his wife. He also spends money in extremes. At times, he lavishes his wife with gifts, and at other times complains that she is spending too much money on groceries. The impact of not feeling good enough to be loved by his mother, also shows up in how D'Andre pressures his two children, especially his son, to be perfect. Because he's always pointing out something that his son did wrong, his son is developing low self-esteem.

Cassaundra has looked only at her own relationship patterns and, as a consequence has lived her life seeing herself as hopelessly damaged. It's great to recognize your emotional patterns. Looking at your pattern without also examining and understanding the patterns in your family system that have shaped you often leads you on a path of hopelessness and self-condemnation. To understand the full picture of what your relationship patterns are telling you, it is important to look at the influences on your worldview, your love narrative, your self-image, and so on that have been shaped by your extended family system. As you do, you become able to use insights about your family system to empower you to change and heal patterns in your life.

While there may be actual details of events and relationships in your family system that you never uncover, it can still transform your life by looking at the patterns in your family to help you understand some of your relationship choices more fully. Knowledge is power. The more you know that the ways you were raised and socialized in your family have impacted the relationship choices you've made in your life, the more you know that you have the power to make different choices. The more you understand why you've felt more comfortable making certain choices that ultimately didn't serve you well, you feel safer to move beyond your comfort zones. You cannot do what you do not know. As you know more, you can do more. As you know that there are more options for your life, the more options you can choose. As you understand more about what has shaped you, you can begin to let go of guilt and shame, and forgive yourself.

Reflection Questions

1. What are the common indicators that you are denying something that you don't want to face? Who can you ask to help you to be honest with yourself?
2. In what ways do you tell yourself—with your words or your actions—that you are broken, damaged, or that something was wrong with you?
3. What coping strategies have you learned from your family? Of these strategies, which work well for your healthy, happiness, and wholeness, and which do you need to let go of?
4. What people or experiences in your life or what beliefs about God do you have that make it difficult for you to forgive yourself?
5. If you want to be more happy, loved, and whole in your life, what do you need to do differently to help you forgive yourself?

Chapter Five

What Is the Spiritual Learning in This for Me?

Everything that irritates us about others can lead us to an understanding of ourselves.

—Carl Jung

On the wings of emotional pain come new possibilities for wholeness. I can't tell you how many times I've said words like these in sermons, counseling sessions, and even to myself. Yet when I experienced the deepest hurt of my life, it was hard for me to access these kinds of life-giving, hope-inspiring words. Despite how much I truly believe them, when I was hurting at my tenderest places, instead of focusing on "the new possibilities for my wholeness," all I could see and feel was my love-hurt. I obsessed on my pain. I was stuck in a loop of my own thoughts. Thoughts that left me feeling anxious, angry, and depressed.

I was confused by what I saw myself doing, how I saw myself thinking. Looping. Most of my life, I have been very effective in focusing on what I need to do to help myself move forward, rather than going around in circles by focusing on what others have said or done to me. I've understood that the actions of others could greatly impact my life, but not determine it. So I was puzzled by my own unproductive, even counter-productive thoughts. I wanted to move forward through the pain, but I could not.

At times I couldn't seem to stop myself from thinking, "My life would be happy, peaceful, and free if only she _____" (whatever I thought she needed to fix in her life) or "Because of him, I am not _____ (whatever I wanted to be in my life)." In the midst of these anxiety-based thoughts, I talked to myself and reminded myself that she didn't have power over my life. I counseled myself that regardless of what he did, I still had the ability to make choices that were right for me. I told myself, "Stop obsessing about them!"

As a counselor, I could clearly see what her issues were that led her to make choices that really hurt me. So I focused on her issues as the sole cause of my pain. Honestly, how does focusing on what someone else needs to do to heal, learn, and grow for their lives really help me move out of my pain? Well, it doesn't.

In the midst of my obsessive self-talk, I imagined what the person who hurt me was doing when we were apart. I made up stuff that left me feeling more unloved and unappreciated than her actual actions. "Stop!" "Stop!" I realized that was a classic example of Albert Einstein's definition of insanity: "doing the same thing over and over again and expecting different results." In that way, my obsessing on the other person was somewhat insane.

I didn't know why I couldn't stop this cycle of counter-productive thinking. It was as if I developed OCD (obsessive-compulsive disorder). I didn't even recognize myself. I was ashamed of myself for not being able to move on. I whined and whined. A whiner, not me? I got on my own nerves. If I could have gotten away from myself, I would have. But the obsessive, depressing thoughts followed me everywhere, even when I was praying or meditating or journaling. "Help me, God, help me!"

Then a voice within me, though I didn't want to listen, kept telling me that staying focused on my love-hurt and on psychologizing the faults and issues of the person who "caused" my pain were not helping to ease my pain. Eventually, I decided to try a different strategy for dealing with my hurt. I focused on me without judgment, criticism, shame, blame, or guilt. I looked at me to understand what I was feeling and why. I worked to understand what it was about the relationship with this particular person or these particular issues that were knocking me so off balance. The ways I saw myself behaving were so uncharacteristic for me. I knew that there must have been some unhealed wounds within me that the current hurt had tapped into deeply. But I didn't know what it was. Only as I let go of self-judgment and shame did I begin to understand what was going on inside me. As my friend Rev. Fred Dennard says, "It's all an inside job Suga!"

What was going on inside me was that I opened myself to be more vulnerable with her than I ever had before with anyone. She tapped into the tenderest places in me, the places where my unhealed wounds were—wounds that were suppressed, blocked, and unknown. I had grown enough to be more vulnerable, it was time for me to learn some new things about myself that could only happen at this deeper level of vulnerability.

Once I started focusing on me instead of what was done to me, I understood that I was at a threshold of possible emotional healing and spiritual growth that I had never come to before. It was the intersection of the love and the pain emerging from the same relationship that brought me to this new threshold. I had to decide whether I would cross the threshold into unknown possibilities for my wholeness and all of the unknowns that might come with that, or return to the safe, familiar ways of relating with others that were my emotional comfort zone. I knew that I didn't want to keep hurting the way I was. I recognized that part of why I was hurting so badly was because I needed to do more healing, learning, and growing.

Ultimately what I experienced was not really about the person who hurt me, but about my own spiritual journey. As I mentioned in Chapter 1 "If You Love Me," in each moment, we are every age we have ever been. In our spiritual journey, who we are now and all of who we have been travel together in a bus (our physical bodies) along the highways and roadways of our lives. A spiritual journey is the collection of experiences and encounters that we (current and all previous ages) have across the course of our lives that challenge and nurture the expression of our vital essence. It is an adventure, treasure hunt, and classroom all rolled up into one. At various points along our journeys, we experience crises, obstacles, and pitfalls of varying enormity and intensity, along with opportunities, possibilities, and miracles. Each experience offers us new resources to go to the next level of healing, growing, and learning as we continue along our journeys.

At the point in my spiritual journey where I was in the midst of the most intense pain of my life, my pain popped my eyes open to see that only as I dared to go through my pain could I cross a threshold into a deeper experience of love. Making this step into love would lead me into greater wholeness. As I began taking this step, I understood four critical things that support me in my spiritual journey: (1) focus on the message, not the messenger; (2) understand the purpose of the relationship, (3) don't confuse the resources with the source, and (4) look behind the mask. Seeing these things gave me the courage I needed to take this step through my pain.

Focus on the Message

God used—not necessarily sent, but definitely used—the pain I experienced and the person I loved to help me uncover some vital things about me that I needed to see and learn. The pain and the person who hurt me were both messengers and teachers bringing critical information to me about me. I had been so focused on the various messengers in my life that I wasn't fully getting the message, so focused on the teachers that I wasn't learning the lesson. The ways that I responded to these messengers and teachers shed important light on what I needed to see about me—my wounds, anxieties, and attachments and on my strengths, potentials, and opportunities.

The woundedness in other people often holds up a mirror to help us to see the brokenness and woundedness in our own lives and a reflection of the things we can become. At a spiritual level, we invite certain people into our lives to help us to heal wounds from our past and to strengthen our emotional and spiritual capacity for our future. The opportunities for growth and healing are often presented by challenge, hardship, and pain. That's why it is often said, "Be careful about praying for patience because that invites having to wait." Of course, we would prefer to pray for something like patience and wake up the next morning and magically have it. But it only comes in the journey and the choices we make along the way. It is a similar process to how diamonds, pearls, and other precious gems are made—friction, pressure, and time. We are being diamondized!

Because your spirit wants to learn, grow, and heal, throughout your life journey, you invite people into your life who have emotional issues that hit your wounded or undeveloped emotional places. They are your spiritual teachers. What your spiritual teachers do is comparable to doctors poking and prodding your body, not to hurt you, but to pinpoint the specific place of pain in order to develop the right plan of treatment. Or teachers who give you tests, not to punish you or show you how stupid you are, but to help you identify what you still need to learn.

The love-hurt you experience brings with it an invitation for you to push beyond your human tendency to react in fear and instead to connect with your divine capacity to respond in love. If you do not recognize and receive the message inviting you to healing, learning, and growing you will keep getting the same message again and again, one painful situation after another. That is, you are likely to "keep dating the same guy, wearing different shoes and different haircut." Watch the patterns of the kinds of pains you have experienced, the patterns of the personalities that keep coming into your life, those are the messages about the things your spirit wants to learn and the areas of healing that your spirit knows that you need.

Here's a story about a woman who didn't recognize what her spirit wanted to learn, and so kept repeating her relationship choices.

Julianna and her father had an incredibly love-hate relationship. It didn't start that way. When she was a little girl, her father Hank doted over her, and she was definitely daddy's little girl. When she became a teenager, everything changed. Julianna who used to worship her father, now saw his flaws and felt free with her dad to point them out. In response to this, Hank became very hurtful to his daughter, smacking her not only with his words, but sometimes with his hands. Often he would be verbally or physically abusive for no apparent reason. She asked her mother Margaret, "Why's dad so mad at me?" Her mother told her that she needed to stop fighting with her father and to try to keep the peace.

Hank's relationship with his son was very different. While he was not very close with his son John, he was always very forgiving of him. Despite his abuse toward Julianna, Hank never spoke a mean word to his son, which deeply hurt his daughter. Because of her hurt, Julianna became more impatient and abrasive toward her father. At other times, trying to keep the peace, she would go for weeks living in the same house but not speaking to him rather than having another fight erupt. Margaret talked with both Hank and Julianna urging them to make peace with one another. But because she did not like dealing with conflict, most of the time Margaret did not intervene, and especially not in the heat of an argument. She put most of the peace-keeping responsibility on her daughter.

Julianna moved out of her family home while she was just 18 years old when she met and moved in with Richard. Richard was 27 when they met. Richard loved to buy expensive gifts for Julianna far more than she was accustomed to receiving. The gifts were not important to her, but the time and attention that Richard gave were wonderful. They spent most of their time alone together and rarely with other people. Richard told her that he liked to have her all to himself. Julianna adored Richard for how gentle he was with her. After she graduated from college and was doing well on her job, Richard started becoming more possessive. Shortly after she graduated, he urged that they have a child. When their daughter Isabella was born, Richard insisted that Julianna quit her job and devote her attention to their daughter, saying, "I don't want strangers raising my child."

Once she stopped working and contributing to the family income, Richard became more controlling. In her effort to keep the peace, Julianna only talked with her family and friends on the phone when Richard was not at home. If she were hanging up the phone as he was coming in the house, he accused her of "talkin' to some man," and would become verbally abusive to her. After they had their second daughter, Richard became more controlling, possessive, and distrustful. One day when her four-year-old daughter asked, "Why is daddy always mad?," Julianna asked herself how she ended up in a relationship with a man who was like her father. She asked, "Is this some cosmic joke or is there something I'm supposed to learn from this?"

Reflection on Story. Julianna's daughter helped her realize more clearly than she had allowed herself to see before that Richard was just as mean to her as her father had been. The two significant men in her life were both Jekyll and Hyde, just as loving and gentle they could be, they could also be mean and abusive. She realized that both men were nicest to her when they felt she was dependent upon them. The more self-reliant she became and the more she related with them as an equal, the more violent they were toward her. In an effort to keep the peace and to avoid the hostility she experienced from her father, for years Julianna didn't speak her mind as freely with her husband. But as she grew fully into her womanhood, it became harder for her not to share her strong opinions. She realized that both men were very insecure. She understood that because of her father's insecurity, he married her mother who wouldn't stand up to him. And because of Richard's insecurity he was initially attracted to her when she was still a young girl who didn't know much and didn't offer much challenge. But why these relationships? If she was meant to learn something, what was it? Once she looks beyond the personalities of Hank and Richard, Julianna can get clarity about the value and purpose of these relationships in her life.

Identifying the Relationship's Purpose

Why did Julianna connect with Richard? Most psychologists generally agree that when we connect with someone like our parents—their best and their worst—it is because unconsciously we are seeking to recreate what is familiar to us and perhaps to resolve issues and heal wounds from those early relationships. Julianna was attempting to heal the pain she experienced with her father.

Sometimes we enter relationships attempting to re-write the story we had with others, especially parents. Julianna had an unconscious hope that by having a different relationship with the same kind of personality as Hank's that would magically cancel out the pain from her relationship with her father.

Why did Julianna come to the particular father and mother that she had—an insecure rage-aholic and a conflict avoider? The spiritual invitation to learn, grow, and heal does not only come in the form of your adult-to-adult relationships. Sometimes the invitation comes into your life while you are still a child. Consider this: Before you were born, your spirit decided upon specific things to learn. The circumstances of your birth, childhood, and the parents you have—through the ways that they were/are present or absent—are the classroom for your learning. The lessons do not always come easy.

Let's consider that Julianna's spirit wants to learn how to create healthy boundaries while at the same time how to establish loving intimacy. The balance of these two ways of relating is not easy for her to learn, or most of us. As a young girl, Julianna only experienced intimacy with her father that was conditioned upon her dependence on and adoration of him. Once she began to individuate and create age-appropriate boundaries for her own personhood, the intimacy was lost. This pattern repeated with Richard to help her spirit to learn this lesson about healthy boundaries and heal from the hurt she experienced from her father. With Richard, Julianna has the opportunity to do the next level of her learning regarding the balance of boundaries and intimacy.

If Julianna's spirit is seeking to learn, grow and heal, how might she proceed in her relationships to accomplish the balance of intimacy and boundaries? It begins not with her father or husband, but with her mother.

Stuck in her anxiety about conflict, Margaret was not able to model for Julianna how to establish the intimacy-boundary balance. In part, because

Margaret did not protect Julianna in the ways that she needed to do for her child's development and for her own learning, Julianna learned early on to defend herself since she knew that her mother would not. Julianna has never acknowledged the anger she has toward her mother. As discussed in Chapter 2 "Why Do I Still Love You," operating with either-or thinking about her feelings toward her mother, Julianna has not been able to let herself know that it is okay for her to be angry at her mother who she loves. She also has not allowed herself to acknowledge that she was even hurt (rear-ended) by her mother's lack of protection. Since she has not allowed herself to know that she's been hurt, she has not been able to heal the hurt.

Because her relationship with her mother is generally a safe and loving relationship, starting with this relationship to strengthen greater balance of intimacy and boundaries will help both Julianna and Margaret to heal and to grow. During Julianna's childhood, because of the conflict-related anxiety that Margaret had, she wanted to quiet her anxiety by urging Julianna to operate with the same unhealthy, "keep the peace at all cost" boundaries that she did.

When Julianna's spirit knew that lack of boundaries did not work for her, she attempted to create something else but she did not know how. Talking with her mother Margaret is the first step for Julianna to take. Even if Margaret does not acknowledge the impact of her conflict-avoidance upon the family relationships, for Julianna speaking her truth to her mother about her experience growing up will greatly help her to practice creating new boundaries. Julianna is likely to wrestle with an impulse not to say anything to Margaret because she doesn't want to hurt her mother's feelings. This impulse is a reflection of the kind of boundaries that Julianna learned from her mother. To push beyond this impulse in a loving way is part of Julianna's spiritual healing and growth and a needed step to prepare her for what she may need to do relating to her father or husband.

Establishing the balance of intimacy and boundaries is not easy with people whose anxiety and emotional woundedness leads them to try to take up all of the space in their relationships and who defend against true intimacy. Yet, Julianna can move toward this balance within herself even if it is not possible in those relationships. In order for Julianna to begin creating more balance in her relationships and within herself, there are seven key steps that will help especially when used on a consistent basis:

1. Remember that the person who hurts her is acting in knee-jerk response to his own pain. Remember that when he strikes out it is an indication that he does not feel safe, special, and respected. He may be expressing his fear of abandonment.
2. Imagine him as a little child experiencing hurt and responding to his anxiety and fear.
3. Imagine herself (little girl to present age) and her loved one (little boy to present age) surrounded by the light of love—a protective force field to block out negativity, fear, and anger and to deepen her experiences of power of love.
4. Shift her focus from what the other person needs to be or do in order for her to be happy to begin exploring what she needs to do for her own happiness and wholeness not contingent upon anyone else.
5. Identify what she needs to heal, without self-judgment, shame and blame.
6. Search for what her spirit is longing to learn through the experience.
7. Recognize any attachments that she may be holding onto because of her own anxiety and assess how these attachments may be blocking her from getting to her wholeness.

Distinguishing Resources from the Source

Theologian Paul Tillich tells us that "everything that is a matter of unconditional concern is made into a god."[4] I have observed that tendency within myself and others to become attached to people and things. Instead of relating with them as resources for love and companionship, challenge and healing, comfort and growth, we relate with them as if they were the Source of our wellbeing and our existence. We conflate and regard the resources and the Source as if they are the same thing. When we conflate and confuse the resources in our lives with the Source of our lives, we become likely to make choices that are directed by our anxiety and fear rather than guided by love and trust. Choices such as: staying in relationships that are killing us spiritually; trying to control and possess our loved ones; relating with others in co-dependent ways without healthy boundaries; living in constant fear of abandonment and disappointment; competing with our loved ones instead of encouraging and supporting them; sabotaging relationships that are the most important and special to us; and compromising our character and integrity in order to stay in our comfort zones with our attachments.

The reason we become attached to those people and things is because our minds believe that only what we can see, touch and feel can truly make us safe, special, and satisfied. That's all our minds know. But there is such an incredible spiritual dimension to who we are that the people and things we make our gods cannot adequately satisfy. The people and things that we become attached to are symbols pointing us toward what we are longing for to quiet our anxieties and satisfy our spirits. Because they can't, we become frustrated and angry at the objects of our attachment for not taking away our anxiety. And we become more anxious. We convince ourselves that if only we had more of those attachments, we would be happy. This anxious belief leads people to have a host of sexual partners, insatiable financial greed, willingness to do anything to gain or maintain a certain social status, and more. We cannot get enough of any of these things to truly give us enough safety, specialness, or satisfaction in our lives.

The resources in our lives, however, do have tremendous spiritual significance by leading us to the Source. They:

1. Point to something beyond themselves and ourselves.
2. Open up levels of spiritual reality that are otherwise closed to us.
3. Unlock dimensions of our spirits which correspond to dimensions of reality yet awaiting us to experience.
4. Cannot be intentionally manufactured the way we want.
5. Grow and die, they come and go.
6. Are created in a specific social context.

The song, "Material Girl," sung by Madonna in the 1980s emphasizes that we live in a material world. While this is true, a more accurate understanding is that we are spiritual beings living in a spiritual world that manifests materially through the things we can hear, see, touch, smell, and feel. We often approach the material as the end all be all of our lives, when in truth, the material world is pointing to something bigger, something spiritual. The material things in our lives are only symbols pointing to that which we cannot experience with our five senses, but with our sixth sense of the spirit. When we become attached to material things and make them the "sources" of our safety and specialness, we live in the anxiety of the potential of losing that which is really only a symbol.

As we recognize that this material world is only a symbol pointing to that which is both who we are and beyond who we are, we encounter the Source and the Essence of all life. This is the path to a deeper level of reality—spirituality—than what can be revealed and understood in the material world. Only the spiritual reality is eternal; all other realities are short-lived and vaporous like dreams. In truth, most often our understanding of reality is backwards, like seeing an image in a mirror. We call reality that which our minds can conceive. But what we call reality is often the figments of our imaginations. Reality is greater than what we can conceive; for it is reality that conceived us.

When we experience eternal spiritual reality, we are transformed. By transformed, I do not mean that we become something that we have not been, rather, we return to our most authentic selves. Encounters with spiritual reality enable us to break through and release our attachments to relationships, social images, traditions and so on that narrowly define us. Releasing these attachments frees us to be who we are without circumscribing and fitting ourselves into the little boxes of "self" that others place us in and the comfort zones that we confuse with safety and security. As we intimately and unashamedly connect with the spiritual reality, that is the Source of our beings, we discover and recover dimensions of ourselves that we have not known or have forgotten.

Anxiously and tenaciously holding onto something or someone that cannot be manufactured into what you want and that inherently grows and dies only exacerbates your anxiety. Connecting with the Source and nurturing your spirit helps you relate in healthy ways with the different resources in your life. As you journey through countless life experiences, angels and ancestors come across your path in various forms to help you recognize your attachments to resources and to redirect you back to the Source. Here is an example of what that might look like in your relationships.

"God, make that man act right!" This was a prayer that Karen spoke often, especially after her boyfriend stayed out all night drinking. Ken used to do that from time to time when they first moved in together. But when Karen moved out once, Ken begged her to come back and promised that he would go to Alcoholics Anonymous meetings. He was going to meetings fairly regularly for almost a year. Karen attended a couple of Ala-non meetings but it brought up too much stuff from her childhood that she didn't want to deal with so she didn't continue going. She was so mad at herself for falling in love with a man who was alcoholic, given that her mother was. Because of all the pain from dealing with her mother's alcoholism, Karen expected that she would have been able to recognize the signs better, but she didn't. She fell in love with Ken on their first date; he swept her off her feet so fast that she didn't have time to see the signs.

When he's not drinking, Ken is everything that Karen has always wanted in a man. He is smart, strong, reliable, and generous. Karen could always count on Ken to figure things out. Ken feels very special being the man Karen depends on. For example, Ken and Karen put their income into one account and Ken handles all of the bills. Karen loves not having to think about anything financial. They live a very comfortable life. Karen's friends tell her that she is spoiled, and that she shouldn't make such a big deal about his drinking from time to time. But for Karen, alcoholism is weakness. Since Ken has started drinking again, Karen doesn't respect him as much as she used to, and she no longer feels as safe. Ken was her rock. Now, she sees him as a drunk.

Ken stopped going to AA meetings so he could work additional hours shortly after they became pregnant. Soon after he started drinking again. While they had talked about having a baby soon, the pregnancy happened sooner than Ken had expected. His drinking was triggered by his fear of all the responsibilities he felt he had. Ken liked that Karen relied on him a lot, but he was also overwhelmed by it. He felt that she criticized and became angry with him for not being perfect. He has never expressed these feelings to Karen. Nor has he told her that he needs her strength too.

Karen is now seven months pregnant. With each month of the pregnancy, Ken's drinking has increased. He stays out more and more. Karen feels completely alone. Lately, she says to Ken that she can't take this anymore and that she wants Ken to leave. Ken refuses to move. Last week, Ken stayed out drinking once again. While he was at work the next day, Karen moved out.

Reflection on Story. Karen relied on Ken for her sense of safety. Because of her attachment to him as her source of safety, she could not tolerate imagining that he too felt scared and weak at times. Essentially, she could not let him be human. Karen has not allowed herself to learn about the kinds of things that can trigger drinking and she looks at alcoholism only through the lens of her childhood pain and judgments about her mother. Though Karen has sought spiritual support, it has not been to help her learn what she needs to learn or grow in the ways she needs to grow, it has only focused on fixing Ken so he can be her anchor. If Karen would focus on her healing and growth, she might be more able to support Ken in doing the healing work that he needs to do for himself.

Ken's sobriety is his choice and his responsibility. To support his recovery, he needs to have open and honest conversations with Karen about creating space in their relationship for them to seek the support of spiritual sources rather than for him to be Karen's source of safety. Ken needs to talk about his safety needs as well. In order for him to have those conversations, Ken has to let go of his attachment to his role and self-image of being Karen's rock.

Like Ken, many of us have been socialized to believe that it is not okay to admit when we feel overwhelmed, anxious or scared. Instead we make use of unhealthy coping mechanisms such as fighting in the relationship, fleeing from it, or emotionally freezing. Activating unhealthy coping strategies are signals not only of stress and grieving, but more specifically, signals of our anxiety about the possibility of losing our attachments in some way or other.

Seeing the pattern of fight, flight or freeze provides the opportunity to inquire what the attachment is telling you about what the other person or yourself are most afraid of losing. Understanding this is the threshold to greater emotional freedom and spiritual wholeness. It is the opportunity to rely more strongly on the Source than on the resources and attachments in your life.

To Thine Own Self Be True

One of the attachments often most challenging to spiritual learning and growth is our social image (reputation, social status, and material wealth). The combination of these attachments is what Carl Jung refers to as persona.[5] Persona is a Latin word that means "mask or character." In psychological terms, persona represents all of the different social masks that you wear as you relate with different groups and in different situations. Persona is how you present yourself to and are perceived by the world.

The purpose of the persona is to shield your ego (your authentic self) from real and perceived negative messages and reactions in the world. Your persona conceals your truest thoughts and feelings and reflects an emotional adaptation of yourself to the outside world. You develop your persona to avoid the potential pain of rejection and abandonment.

The persona develops in ways that help you to feel safe and special as you navigate the uncertainties of human relationships and of life. Persona is the mask that you wear to be accepted by the individuals and in the groups that you feel will most give you love, nurture, and safety. Children develop personas to please their parents in order to receive the affirmation that they need. Employees develop personas in their workplaces to be perceived as team players or leaders to position themselves for promotions. Religious adherents in their places of worship or spiritual practice take on certain personas that are regarded as righteous, saved or godly in order to be embraced by the spiritual community and by God.

I say that persona is one of the greatest challenges to spiritual learning and growth because as you operate with the social mask, you can begin to lose a true understanding of who you really are. Your social image begins to meld with your self-image to which you can become attached to provide our sense of safety and specialness.

Because your persona guides how you show up in relationships, true intimacy that goes behind the surface of the mask, character, or role can feel like a tremendous risk to open yourself to be seen in your authenticity. An authenticity that you might not even have clarity about yourself. Taking the risk of being intimate with others is vital to spiritual learning and growth because it invites others to hold a mirror up to you so that you can see yourself clearly unmasked.

For many of us, the fear of what might happen and how we might be perceived if we truly let go of the mask is so overwhelming that we rather fight, flee or freeze than to be seen. So we cling to the attachments of social image that the persona holds in place for us.

Here is an example of what became possible in Julianna's life when she looked behind the mask of her social image:

> As Julianna became more consciously aware of how emotionally controlling and verbally abusive her husband Richard was, she was too embarrassed to discuss this with

anyone. She was known in her family for being very direct and has the courage to stand up to anyone. She didn't want to be perceived in any other way. She kept wondering how she had let herself get in this relationship. She insisted to herself, "I am not a victim."

Both Julianna and Richard were very involved in their church. Since Richard was not willing to go to see a marriage counselor, she thought about going by herself to see their pastor for counseling. But for a long time she wrestled with feeling too vulnerable. As Richard continued to escalate his possessiveness and control, and as her daughter continued to ask why her daddy was so mad, eventually, Julianna went to talk with her pastor.

The path into spiritual wholeness and emotional wellbeing calls you to know that it is okay to let down your mask and to know that you are safe and special and loved. Hear that call within your spirit and say yes.

Expectations, Anxieties and Spiritual Paradoxes

"I did it! I prayed for those people who've been so mean to me. I can't explain it, but I really do feel better. I feel more peaceful and calm." A few years prior to this testimony, Yolanda had told me about a situation on her job that was filling her with heartache and anger every day. When I urged her to pray for the people who seemed to be going out of their way to make her life miserable, she responded, "Hell no!" So it was a great joy when she told me that she had finally prayed for them and that she recognized the positive difference it made for her.

Whether or not you pray for others who have hurt you, the point is to make the choice to stay rooted in love, no matter what others may say or do to you. In that way, loving others like you've never been hurt is the greatest gift you can give to yourself.

Because loving like this is a spiritual paradox, it may seem like the opposite of what your mind may tell you to do. Spiritual paradoxes are those things that our intellects tell us will lead us away from what we want for they seem to be the opposite of what makes rational sense.

Spiritual paradoxes are highlighted across spiritual traditions to guide us in our relationships and love. For example,

- "Never retaliate in kind. Hatred does not come to an end through hatred but can only cease through generosity." (Buddhism, *Jataka Tale*)
- "Bless those who curse you." (Christianity, *Holy Bible*)

And there are spiritual paradoxes about how to interpret life and see yourself. For example,

- "Within tears, find a hidden laughter; seek treasure amid ruins, sincere one." (Islam, *Mathnawi*)
- Yesterday I lived bewildered, in illusion. But now I am awake, flawless and serene, beyond the world. From my light, the body and the world arise. So all things are mine, or nothing is." (Hinduism, *Ashtavakra Gita*)
- "We do not see things as they are; we see things as we are." (Judaism, *Talmud*)
- "Defects in your character, when suppressed or ignored, continue. But when allowed to be present in your awareness, they wither away." (Taoism, *Tao te-Ching*)

But how do you know what is a spiritual paradox versus what is fantasy thinking? Pay attention to the results inside you. Fantasy thinking leaves you anxious and resentful because you still do not have the sense of safety and peace that you were seeking. When you follow the principles of spiritual paradoxes, however, you experience the kind of peace and calm described by Yolanda in the opening sentences of this chapter. Following the guidance of spiritual paradoxes deepens your joy even though you can't explain it or understand it.

Here's how spiritual paradoxes work. When you become attached to specific resources in your life—money, social image, house, lover, coping strategies, etc., you are likely to develop expectations of what those resources will or should provide for you to "make" you happy, safe, and special. Or you can feel anxious about the possibility of the things and people you are attached to being taken away. As your anxiety mounts and your stress grows, your perceptions of reality become distorted. Expectations flip you sideways and anxieties turn you upside down. You flip and flop every which way, but up.

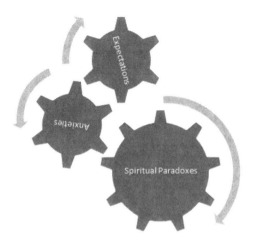

That's when you are most likely to act in knee-jerk reaction and hurt those who are closest to you and also end up hurting yourself. The love-like-you've-never-been-hurt spiritual paradox is an antidote to the effects of expectations and anxieties. It's an antidote that turns the world right side up again. So while spiritual paradoxes appear to be upside down, they are really recalibrating and realigning your perceptions to see yourself, others, and the situations you're in more clearly and fully, right-side-up. Spiritual paradoxes help you move through the human tendency to self-protect and your pattern to fight, flee or freeze.

Reflection Questions

1. Who do you tend to psychologize and whose issues do you tend to blame for you not being as satisfied in your life as you want to be? Instead of focusing on them and their issues, what messages are they giving to you about you and what you need to learn or heal?
2. When you see yourself focusing on your pain or the person who hurt you, what would help you to focus on you?
3. Think about the joys and challenges you have experienced with your parents and immediate family. Why might your spirit have selected them as your family and your teachers? What are they in your life to help you learn?

4. Describe your persona—how you present yourself to others. In what ways do you cling to your persona to help you feel safe, respected, and special? How might this impede your spiritual growth?
5. What resources in the material world do you at times rely upon as the sources for your wellbeing?
6. What attachments and anxieties have turned your perceptions sideways and your life upside-down? What spiritual paradox do you need to embrace to turn your life right-side-up?

Chapter Six

How Do I Take Care of Me?

Know yourself, and give yourself what you need.
—Cari Jackson

In response to the saying, "Time heals all wounds," Rose Kennedy said, "I do not agree. The wounds remain. In time, the mind, protecting its sanity, covers them with scar tissue and the pain lessens. But it is never gone."

The mere passage of time alone cannot heal your loved-related pain. To heal the emotional wounds of love-hurts requires focused intention. Intentional time is a period in which you give purposeful and deliberate attention to your thoughts, words, and actions focused on the goal of healing.

It is often a challenge to make the intentional time to do the work of healing. When you are hurting from a love-hurt, you want to things to stop or slow down—job responsibilities, the care of your children or parents, school assignments, health concerns you have, community or religious activities—so that you can attend to your pain. You want time to lick your wounds, get under the covers in the bed, you want to be left alone, or you want people to care for you without you having to say what you need or anything about what's going on within your heart. But that rarely happens. Life and its demands keep going on.

Since the passage of time alone cannot heal you, how do you take care of yourself in the midst of your pain and all that is expected or demanded of you? It starts with knowing yourself and giving yourself what you need.

Not merely at the surface level, such as your need for a vacation or need not to talk with certain people, but at the level of what underlies those needs.

Healing Words

The beauty about intentional time is that even when you do not have time to take specific actions that help you heal, you can still attend to your thoughts and the words you speak about yourself and your vision for your life. The more intentional—that is, deliberate and purposeful—you are about what you focus your thoughts on and what you speak, you can heal your wounds and old scar tissue.

In biblical Hebrew, dabar means speech, word, or thing. Dabar reminds us that there is a creative power in what we speak. According to Judeo-Christian scripture, humanity is created in the image of God who spoke the world into existence. That means that we have the power to create by what we speak. What we speak matters for it both shapes and manifests in our lives in one way or other.

The most important aspect of how you engage intentional time to heal is what you speak. The words you speak about yourself, the person who brought the hurt, the hurtful situation, and your overall life impact your healing in three ways.

First, when you are hurting, if your words are filled with shame, self-judgment and condemnation, such as, "You're so stupid" or "You messed up again," you are likely to feel weak, powerless, and hopeless. If your words about the person who hurt you are filled with blame, such as, "He ruined my life," you are likely to feel that your life really is ruined. To help yourself to heal, pay attention to what you speak for your words do have the power to create love, hope, and new possibilities or fear, anger, and resignation to pain.

Second, in addition to having a creative capacity, what you speak is critical because it helps reveal to you what you're thinking. Your thoughts are really where your healing begins. Often you might not even know what you're thinking until you hear yourself say certain things. Talking out loud to yourself, in a conversation with a loved one or counselor, or writing in a journal helps you get clear about what you're thinking. The kinesthetic process of using your body (whether talking, writing long-hand, or typing into a computer) to find the words to articulate your feelings greatly assists you to discover and explore your thoughts.

As you have more clarity about what you're thinking and why, you can assess whether those thoughts support you in your healing. If they don't, you can focus deliberately in changing your thoughts by "crowding out" unproductive, life-demoting thoughts with productive life-promoting ones. It is easier to replace unsupportive thoughts with supportive ones than it is to stop thinking. Which is why simply saying, "I just won't think about that anymore," rarely works. Instead, create some words that reflect what you want for yourself and say those words throughout the day. Subvocalize, not just think, but say softly to yourself the words that you choose to guide your life. Speak them in the shower, walking down the street, driving the car, washing dishes, using the computer. Whatever you do throughout your day, speak the words to retrain and reprogram your thoughts.

Why subvocalize and not just think the words? For two reasons. As you engage your body in this retraining process, you create a kinesthetic body memory in association with the supportive words to transform and heal your life. Each time you speak words about yourself and about your life, you send electrical waves that create particular neurological pathways in your brain. Over time with repeated use of certain words and thoughts, your brain becomes trained to access these well-used pathways. Whatever you generally speak about yourself, whether hurtfully or lovingly, those are the pathways of neurological synaptic connections that are most likely to occur. That is, whatever you tend to speak about yourself every day, when you are hurting that is what your brain is already trained to think about you. If you've generally been filling yourself with negative thoughts, you can use your intentional time for healing to begin to develop some new neurological pathways in your brain. To do so requires that you subvocalize words of hope and healing throughout the day to reprogram your thoughts. As you do, your body internalizes healing thoughts, and you begin to heal in mind, body, and spirit.

Third, what you speak also greatly shapes your actions. Each time you speak words that reflect the vision you have for yourself, you strengthen your commitment to achieve that vision. You gain clarity for what you need for your life to realize your vision. As you speak, you engage in a comparative analysis of what your life looks like now and what you seek for yourself. You begin to reflect on your degree of satisfaction in the specific areas of your life. As you focus on your vision for how you want to treat for yourself and be treated by others, consciously and unconsciously you begin to develop plans and strategies for how to fulfill your life vision for various areas of your life. As your plans develop, your actions follow.

Caring for yourself begins with what you speak and think. Then you must make choices about how to have your actions following through on what you say you want and need for you.

Dare to Self-Care

For many of us, the concept of self-care is associated with self-indulgence. Many of us feel guilty about taking time away from our responsibilities, unless we escape fantasy-thinking or denial and engage in one of our unhealthy coping behaviors. Our unhealthy coping strategies ultimately add to the sense of being off balance already begun by the love-hurt.

When you're off balance, you do not make the best choices for your life. To help you to make healthy life-affirming choices to heal your pain, use the opportunity that the love-hurt brings to take a closer look at your life and assess the areas of your life that need your attention and care. To help prepare yourself to take an honest look at all areas of your life, not just the relationship that is the seat of your emotional pain, it is helpful to understand the role and benefits of self-care.

Self-care is a set of loving choices that you make to nurture, support, and care for yourself in various areas of your life to strengthen your wellbeing and wholeness. Self-care is not the common knee-jerk reactions to pain that you might be inclined to use—such as "retail therapy," drinking, eating, having extra-marital affairs, gambling, hoarding, burying in work, and "social media therapy"—which often bring another set of pains and consequences to deal with or that leave you feeling even more broken.

Once you assess the areas of your life that you are very satisfied or unsatisfied with, self-care is the process that you can use to enhance your satisfaction and happiness in each of these areas. Because self-care is focused nurture it will help you feel stronger to deal with the pain and give you more clarity about how you need to handle the situation. Here are some other benefits of self-care:

- Helps you to return to emotional balance more easily after a major upset
- Helps you to distinguish your own issues from those of others
- Enables you to be emotionally present with others
- Enables you to be more effective in your analysis and problem-solving

- Enhances your creativity
- Enhances your clarity
- Helps you to be more patient with yourself and others
- Increases your energy and stamina
- Enables you to stay in touch with your own thoughts and feelings
- Helps strengthen your perspective that life is manageable
- Lowers your stress and improves your physical health
- Helps you stay open to love
- Helps you to enjoy life even in the midst of your pain
- Enhances your attitude of gratitude
- Helps you to feel more free and strong

Identify other benefits of self-care you might experience that will help you deal with your love-hurt and improve the overall quality of your life. And focus on these things, and give thanks.

Areas of Life Satisfaction

Through the years, as I have encouraged people to look at the degree to which they are satisfied with their lives, many have resisted. On some level, they have known that they are not satisfied with their lives and don't want to face it for fear that they would be overwhelmed by what they see. For fear that if they really see, they would feel compelled to make some significant changes they don't feel ready to make. Many of us live with the "I don't want to know" approach to life. This approach keeps us stuck in lives that are under-satisfying and less than happy, yet complaining about not being happy. It is this kind of thinking that keeps us stuck in inaction and locked in pain.

Perhaps instead of presuming that you will be overwhelmed, imagine yourself getting freed and empowered by the clarity you gain about yourself and what you need. Remember, the pain you are experiencing brings with it life-giving messages to help you heal, learn, and grow. And you do not have to do this work by yourself, Divine Spirit is with you. And there are angels and ancestors with you supporting you in your journey into wholeness and joy.

Angels are spiritual beings who serve as agents, messengers or attendants from God dispatched to you to help you. *Ancestors* are loved ones who have physically died but whose spirits are still journeying with you to support and encourage you. Both angels and ancestors are available to support you and help you gain greater clarity about which direction to move in or course of action to take toward greater wholeness and happiness for your life satisfaction. They don't do anything for you, but with you. When you are clear about what you're ready and willing to do, your ancestors and angels are on the J-O-B. to support your success and strengthen your action.

Often we tend to think in terms of life satisfaction in an either-or fashion—either I'm happy or I'm not. This approach does not give you enough information to help you know what you need to focus on, especially when you are hurting. The following breakout of eight life areas can help you appreciate where your resources of joy and support may be and help you focus on changes you may choose to make. This information is to assist you in focusing on ways you can show love to yourself in the midst of your pain.

Areas of Life	*Definitions*
Emotional	Identifying your feelings and using them as resources to make conscious, healthy choices in all areas of your life
Familial/Relational	Strengthening intimacy in your relationships with your partner/spouse, child(ren), parent(s), sibling(s), close friends that are mutually nurturing
Financial	Acquiring and using money as a life resource, without regarding its presence/absence to be the source of your identity or worth
Intellectual	Engaging in activities and projects that stimulate your mental abilities and keep your mind fresh, alert, and open to new learning
Physical	Giving regular care to your body through exercise and healthy eating, especially in light of life stresses and family health history

Professional/ Creational	Engaging your unique abilities to envision, express, interpret, and create in ways that nurture you and enhance other's lives
Social/Recreational	Enjoying recreation, entertainment, and fun activities with friends and family
Spiritual	Nurturing your core self in ways that help you recognize your oneness with the Sacred

Here is an example of how one man examined his life to help him lessen his love-hurt and heal his emotional wounds.

Katarina and Ivan have been married for 22 years. Their marriage was arranged by their families. Katarina was in love with another man but married Ivan to please her parents. Although they had four children together and have become family for one another, they have never shared an intimate, passionate love. Katarina has been a dutiful wife, but has been waiting for the youngest child to graduate from high school so that she could leave Ivan and be happy. The youngest is now 12.

Ivan has been a good provider but has not ever let himself be emotionally vulnerable and intimate with Katarina primarily because he felt that she didn't really love him. While he is tender and loving with his children, he does not give that to his wife. Instead because he has felt rejected by Katarina all of these years, he has been harsh and criticizing toward her.

A few years ago, Katarina figured out that Ivan was seeing another woman. This hurt Katarina, but at least now Ivan has stopped asking her to have loveless sex with him. Ivan is staying out later to avoid coming home. Katarina feels more and more disrespected. She is angry at her family for making her marry a man who she did not love, angry at Ivan for not being someone she could fall in love with, angry at her children for not being older so that she could leave Ivan, and angry at herself for staying in this situation. Because she's been angry so long, she feels herself becoming bitter. For this reason, Katarina finally decided that she would no longer wait until her youngest child was out of high school.

I pause in this story to reflect on Katarina's decision. Based on the information in this story, Katarina's decision to stop the pain she is experiencing in her relationship with Ivan makes a lot of sense. It appears that Katarina has focused solely on the marriage as she has looked at how unhappy she is. And that's what most of us do—focus on the apparent source of our pain. It does not appear that she also looked at other areas of her life to assess the relative ways they add to or take away from her satisfaction and wholeness.

The day Katarina was scheduled to meet with a divorce lawyer, Ivan had a severe stroke affecting his ability to walk, use his right arm, and speak. Katarina felt so trapped that she could hardly speak. She believed her children would never forgive her if she divorced him now and is worried what would happen to Ivan. As Katarina cares for Ivan during his rehabilitation, she shuts down emotionally even more than she has already done. Ivan sees the sadness in her eyes and he knows it is not empathy for him.

During his six-month stay in the rehabilitation center, Ivan began to think about his life. He put up a façade of happiness for so long that he had started to believe that. He convinced himself that the only reason he was seeing another woman was because of the lack of sexual intimacy between him and Katarina. But when he looked at the situation more honestly, for the first time he admitted to himself that he unhappy with much of his life not just his marriage. He made a commitment to himself that he was going to make the changes he needed to be happy.

He established a routine for himself to reflect on his life. Everyday following his therapy exercises, he assessed different areas of his life. He assessed what things in his life really give him joy, not just comfort, but real joy. He recognized that there were very few things in his life that gave him joy: his kids, painting which he stopped doing years ago, making people laugh, and cooking with Katarina. Now that he was unable to work, he admitted how much he didn't like his job. He also admitted to himself that he didn't like himself for cheating on his wife and other ways he had disrespected her. As Ivan used his time in the rehab center to learn more about himself, he became kinder to Katarina, always appreciating the ways that she cared for him. He wondered if there could have been more passion and connection in their relationship all these years if he had not held himself back from her because of his fear of being rejected by her. He realized that he loved Katarina more than he had let himself know.

Shortly before he was scheduled to return home, Ivan asked Katarina if she were happy in their marriage. She asked, "Why are you asking that now?" Ivan slowly shared with her all that he had been thinking. Now that it was hard for him to speak, he shared more openly and honestly than he ever had. He told her that he loved her and that he wanted her to be happy. He urged her that if she were still in love with the man she did not marry years ago, to find him and have the life she always wanted.

Katarina assumed that Ivan must have found out somehow that she was planning to divorce him and that he was only saying these things so that he would not have to pay alimony. "How did you find out?" she said. After a few rounds of questions back and forth, Katarina realized that he did not know her plans. She realized that he was being sincere. Ivan told her, "I know I have hurt you a lot. It was because I knew you loved another man. But that was no excuse. You still deserved better from me. And who knows, maybe if I had been more loving to you, you might have loved me." Katarina responded, "I used to wish you looked at me the way you look at our children—with a tender love. That's all I ever wanted from you. I wanted you to love me, but all I got from you was anger." From that day, Katarina and Ivan began talking more honestly than ever. One day, she took the risk of telling Ivan the things that she does love and appreciate about him. When she did, for the first time ever, they held each other and cried together.

Reflection on Story. In the course of assessing his happiness, Ivan was able to understand why he and Katarina did things that were hurtful to one another, but he remained focused on his actions. As he did, he accepted that his own fears of rejection had blocked what he could have had with a wonderful woman. He didn't blame her for not loving him. Now he is working to forgive himself as he understands that he reacted in the ways he did because he didn't feel safe and special. And he knows that somehow he must make amends to Katarina.

As Ivan looked at his life and how much he appreciates his children, painting, cooking with Katarina, and so on, it made him more determined to work hard at his recovery so that he could return to the things that brought him joy. Ivan recognized that working at a job that was not satisfying because of the constant stress and competition in his work made it even more challenging for him to feel safe enough take emotional risks with Katarina.

What might Ivan and Katarina's relationship have been if one or both of them had had the courage to look at their whole lives, not just the pain from their relationship? What might be the impact on their children given that they did not look honestly at their degree of life satisfaction sooner? Now that they have begun this process of reflection, how might they enhance their children lives going forward? The possibilities await Ivan and Katarina's discovery.

Like Ivan, many of us wait until a crisis overtakes and changes our lives before we examine how satisfied we really are with our lives. But why wait until then? Many of us, like Ivan and Katarina slide into low levels of satisfaction with our lives—one hurt on top of another—before we assess the impact of one hurt another is upon us. We wait for time to do its magic and heal us, but instead only scar tissue forms over the wound. Healing from wounds and learning more about what our deepest needs are take intentional reflection and purposeful action.

It is important to ask yourself how happy you are with each area of your life and what you are willing to do differently to experience the life you long for. Engaging in this self-assessment, looking at each area of your life on its own will help you appreciate the joys that are there. Remember that emotional pain can eclipse the things that are resources of joy for you. The more you remind yourself to see and appreciate those resources and the miracles in your life love fills you and strengthens you.

Being able to see what the overall areas of satisfaction are in your life can give you greater insight into what may make the emotional injury you experienced less daunting and overwhelming. It can help you identify other areas of your life that are unsatisfying and that lower your ability to deal with pains you experience. Exploring your relative satisfaction can help you look at the picture of your life with the goal of understanding and seeing things clearly without guilt, blame and shame.

But what if the person who hurt you is your closest friend? How do you take care of yourself when the person you would ordinarily talk and process things with to help you heal from hurts is also the one who hurt you and betrayed you? How wise is it to expose yourself even further and potentially give her more who and that she might use against you later? These are critical questions to ask. This is a special time to seek your angels and ancestors for guidance because of your pain, it's hard to see clearly. Read Chapter 8 "Why, Who, and How Do I Trust Again?" for more specifics.

As You Think

One of the greatest challenges in love is to establish and maintain healthy boundaries. Love draws us into connection with others. And if we are not awake and aware, we can slide into co-dependence, possessiveness, taking others for granted, fear of abandonment, and more. And when we experience love-related hurt, we often swing to the polar opposites of intimacy and distancing. Our emotional pendulum swings wildly and widely between these two ways of relating. The relationship boundaries become more complicated and erratic. As we may be seeking to create something different for ourselves so that we won't hurt, our thoughts bounce back and forth between self-protection and hope of real connection. For this reason, taking care of yourself in the midst of heartache necessitates looking at what you are thinking, not just about the pain you are going through, but your overall way of looking at the world and processing life so that you can make conscious choices instead of flip-flopping in each moment.

The Book of Deuteronomy in the Holy Bible reflects the story of a community of people who had been in the midst of a painful transition for over a generation. They had experienced a lot of pain, first as they were oppressed in Egypt and then as they sojourned in the wilderness. Egypt had begun like so many relationships, welcoming and embracing, and then things soured in a big way. After getting out of that abusive relationship, they floundered for a long while, scared to believe that the possibilities that they had heard Spirit tell them about in a new place really could be. Having come through catastrophic pain, they were self-protective as they imagined all that it would take to claim what they had been promised. They needed intentional time and intentional strategies to let go of or at least lessen the imprint of the pains they had experienced. They had to find a new way of being in the world, and a new way of relating with God and one another.

Before they were about to cross the physical threshold into a new land, they also had to cross a threshold of thinking—from their old ways of thinking into new ways. This was the threshold where love and pain, danger and opportunity intersect. Their leader, Joshua, spoke with the entire community about the choices they needed to make as they continued the next leg of their transition. Joshua gave them a message from God, "See, I set before you today life and prosperity, death and destruction . . . This day I call heaven and earth as witnesses that I have set before you life and death, blessings and curses. Now choose life, so that you and your children may live."[6]

Divine Spirit knew that if the people's thinking about the future was confined by the hurt, pain, and loss that they have experienced they would not be able to recognize and seize the new possibilities of life that lie ahead of them. Joshua urged them to expand their thinking and choose life, and then to pass that expanded way of thinking onto their children and others whose lives they influence.

Worldview and Choices

Nothing shapes your choices more than your worldview. In Chapter 2 "Why Do I Still Love You?", I introduced the concept of "love narrative," the story you write about love that guides the choices you make in your relationships. Your love narrative stems from your overall thinking about life, or your worldview. Your worldview is the particular philosophy of life or concept of the world that helps you make sense of and interpret what you hear, observe or experience in life. Your worldview holds things together for you in a way that aids you in navigating life. Your worldview is shaped your education, exposure, and experience. Your education is comprised of what you are taught by your family, friends, religion, and school. Your exposure includes what you are exposed to in the books and magazines you read, the news media you listen to and watch, and popular culture. Your experience reflects the range of occurrences and feelings in your own life.

When you are hurting, sad or scared, you rely heavily on your worldview to help make sense of what you are going through. If your worldview is, "the world is not a safe place" or that "everyone is out for themselves," your love narrative is likely to that "men can't be trusted" or the "women just want you for your money" or "parents only want to dictate how you should live" and so on. To help take care of yourself as you are going through your love-hurt, looking at, evaluating, and updating your worldview can be a tremendous way of easing your pain. Engaging in this reflection will help you to identify ways of thinking that keeps you feeling broken, hopeless, and stuck and that limits your sense of what is possible.

Everyone in pain becomes self-protective in one way or other, for a short-term or long-term. If you already lived with the thinking that you need to self-protect, even before you were hurt, you are likely to become more self-protective once hurt. You are likely to feel that there is no one with whom you can share the deepest of your pain. Then self-protection can become scar tissue covering your emotional wound, which if it forms too quickly, can result in impeding your healing and fostering your lingering pain.

If your worldview is "we are all connected" or "even if things are not easy, all will be well," even though you may naturally become self-protective at first, you will be able to reflect on your life to gain more clarity about what you need to do to take care of yourself in ways that are for you and others.

Most of us don't sit around thinking about what our worldview is. To get a clearer sense of yours, look at the choices you make in your life, and ask yourself what patterns there are in your relationship choices and what those patterns indicate about what you believe about life and people. Look at any tendency you may have for co-dependency, a tendency to focus on the needs of the other person more than on your own. Or see your narcissism, a tendency to expect everyone and everything to cater to you. What do these patterns tell you about your love narrative and your overall worldview?

To help you take care of yourself as you deal with and heal from love-hurt, learn more about yourself—what your worldview is, how satisfied you are with various aspects of your life, what you need to feel more whole. Use your pain to know yourself and give yourself what you need to become more happy, free and whole. What you think and what you speak are what you create for your life.

Reflection Questions

1. Think about patterns of relationships, jobs, religious beliefs, etc. that run through your life. In one sentence describe your love narrative. In another sentence describe your overall worldview.
2. How have past hurts influenced your love narrative and worldview? To what extent does your thinking about love and life reflect

unhealthy scar tissue? How does your thinking help or hinder you in choosing life?

3. How can you use the hurts of your life to give you more clarity about what you want for your life?

4. How satisfied are you with each of the areas of your life? (0=not at all satisfied, 4= highly satisfied)

Life Areas		Satisfaction (0-4)	Choices	Messages
Emotional	Identifying your feelings and using them as resources make conscious, healthy choices in all areas of your life			
Familial/ Relational	Strengthening intimacy in your relationships with your partner/ spouse, child(ren), parent(s), sibling(s), close friends that are mutually nurturing			
Financial	Acquiring and using money as a life resource, without regarding its presence/ absence to be the source of your identity or worth			

Intellectual	Using various media and activities to keep your mind fresh, alert and open to new learning			
Physical	Giving regular care to your body, especially in light of family health history and life stresses			
Professional/ Creational	Engaging your unique abilities to envision, express, interpret, and create in ways that nurture you and enhance other's lives			
Social/ Recreational	Enjoying recreation, entertainment, and fun activities with friends and family			
Spiritual	Nurturing your core self in ways that help you recognize your oneness with the holy			

5. What choices do you make that support or impede your satisfaction in each area?

6. What messages did you receive during childhood that influence the choices you make in each area? From whom?

7. If you were fully satisfied with all areas of your life, describe what your life would look like.

8. Select 1-2 life areas to focus on. What do you need to do differently in each of these areas to foster greater wholeness and satisfaction in your life? What are you ready to do differently?

9. What impediments are there in your life to make the needed changes? How can you address these?

10. What supports are present in your life to make these changes? How might you use these supports more effectively?

Chapter Seven

How Do I Heal Past Hurts?

You cannot prevent the birds of sorrow
from flying over your head,
but you can prevent them
from building nests in your hair.

—Chinese Proverb

Love-hurts happen in everyone's lives. They are the birds of sorrow that fly over our heads. We have limited to no control over this reality. What we do have a great deal of control over is whether or not we allow those birds to nest in our lives. When we stay in self-protection, in one way or other in effort to avoid potential hurts, we give the birds of sorrow permission to take up residence in our lives.

Self-protection is a human survival response to love-hurt. Self-protection reflects the anxiety that we feel about being vulnerable to pain again. We self-protect in the various ways we fight, flee, or emotionally freeze. There are three primary reasons that we cling to self-protection: (1) we don't know we're grieving and how to move through it, (2) we become attached to the pain, and (3) we haven't forgiven ourselves or others.

Good Morning, Good Mourning

In the song, "Good Morning, Heartache,"[7] first made famous by jazz legend Billie Holiday, we hear the ballad of someone who is in the midst of profound love-hurt. The song begins by expressing a struggle to let go of the heartache—

> *Good morning heartache*
> *You old gloomy sight*
> *Good morning heartache*
> *Thought we said goodbye last night*
> *I turned and tossed 'til it seemed you had gone*
> *But here you are with the dawn*

Reflecting the weariness experienced from the pain itself, the song ends with surrender to the continued presence of the heartache—

> *. . . Good morning heartache*
> *You're the one who knew me when*
> *Might as well get used to you hanging around*
> *Good morning heartache*
> *Sit down.*

Pain is fatiguing. It wears you down because love-hurt brings an intense grieving. You grieve the death of what you had believed the relationship was or hoped it would become. You grieve the image you had of the person who hurt you or the image you had of yourself. And you don't have much energy to do anything other than surrender to and sit down with the pain.

Sometimes love-hurt knocks you down. Not just a flesh wound, but hits deep into your bones or major organs. When you are reeling from a hit like that—being betrayed at work by your friend, your spouse having an affair while you are battling cancer, repeated abuse or neglect by your parents, or your child stealing a priceless family heirloom—it feels that the only way to get through life is to accept the sadness and pain.

When you don't have the energy to let go of the pain, can't imagine the pain ending, or don't know how to let it go, you are likely to make accommodations for it. Accommodations like not going out with friends for your weekly game or lunch, not decorating your house for what used to be your favorite holiday, or planning that you will be too tired to do your favorite things. Each of these accommodations sends the signal to the heartache to stay and to the birds of sorrow to nest. So how do you get the energy to move through and release the pain and begin to heal?

Recognize That You Are Grieving

The word "grieve" is from the Latin gravare (same root for the word gravity) which means "to burden." Grieving is heavy. That's what makes love-hurt so tiring and exhausting. It's like trying to drive uphill with a very heavy carload on slippery roads at night or in the fog. The load is heavy, you are slipping and sliding, and you can't see well how to proceed. All of this together makes you very disoriented and weary. Here is an example of what the weight and disorientation of grieving can look like.

> A few years ago, shortly before Christmas, my mother Gladys died. My father Robert died 22 years prior. Now I was experiencing the grief of being parent-less. I was grieving big time. In the midst of my grieving, I was responsible for leading a lot of Christmas-related worship and other activities in the church and community where I served as pastor. I was surrounded by songs like "Joy to the World," and signs of Christmas cheer everywhere when my heart was breaking. To get through this I had to discover what I needed to do to take care of myself as I grieved.
>
> Earlier in my life, I would have been so focused on trying to take care of other people by not letting them know how much I was hurting, to not to put a damper on their Christmas joy. After all, I was the pastor and wasn't I supposed to take care of them? I had to push through my fear of being perceived as not being a good pastor and strong person of faith unable to barrel through my grief. Then I realized that part of how I could care for people was by letting them care for me when I am in pain. I allowed myself to vulnerable and honest about my pain. At the Christmas Eve service as the choir sang, "O Holy Night," which was one of the solos my mother used to sing, I allowed myself to cry. As my congregation saw me grieve and as I allowed them to minister to me, not only did I feel loved and strengthened, but the congregation grew stronger in its capacity to care for others. Together, we broke through the either-or paradigms of sorrow or joy to experience the freeing power of joy and sorrow.

Reflection on Story. Being fully present with my grieving did not impede me in my preaching or other forms of ministry. On the contrary, because

I was more open to receiving support from Spirit and the congregation, my ministry became more powerful and effective. Yup! It's one of those spiritual paradoxes: When we acknowledge that we are weak, we become strong. As expressed in the song, "Good Morning, Heartache," I had to acknowledge that I was fatigued and pained by my grieving. As I did, I was able to make some important intentional choices, the first of which was to ensure that I did not hide behind my mask, the persona of pastor. In addition to seeking the support of angels and ancestors to help strengthen me, I was also blessed to angels in bodily form. The support I received only happened as I acknowledged that I needed help.

I recognize that when you are grieving from the hurt of what feels like a betrayal in love that it might not feel comfortable or appropriate to share publicly anything about the pain you are experiencing. But regardless of your circumstance, it is helpful to understand that you are grieving. Allowing yourself to let go of your persona and role can give you helpful insight about what you need to care for yourself.

Recognize What You Value

There are a few different theories about the stages and cycles of grieving that might be useful to help you understand what you are feeling. The first was developed by psychiatrist Elisabeth Kübler-Ross,[8] who proposed Five Stages of Grieving: denial, bargaining, anger, depression, and acceptance. Among the many other models of grieving, another was developed by Colin Parkes and Robert Weiss,[9] who proposed that we move from numbness-denial to yearning to disorganization-despair.

More recent research about grieving, since the stage models of Kübler-Ross and others, suggests that while there are some common experiences in how people grieve there are also some significant differences. These differences are based on specific factors about who we are and how we value our particular losses. For example, a woman who never wanted to be married or have children and whose husband initiates a divorce and seeks custody of their children grieves differently from a man for whom his family is a sign of his success and his wife initiates a divorce and seeks custody of the children. Even if the both the woman and the man who are served the divorce papers were routinely inconsiderate and disrespectful to their respective spouses, because the value they attach to the marriage is different, along with differences in their personalities, they are likely to grieve differently.

So much of how you grieve when you experience love-hurt is influenced by the meaning and the value you have given to the relationship—that is, what the relationship represents for you. Here is a story to illustrate this point.

Dae-Ho and Alanzo have been together for nine years. Two years ago, when marriage became available for same-gender couples, Alanzo began pressing upon Dae-Ho that they get married. Dae continued to resist the idea, asking, "What do we need that for? You know I love you." Each time they have discussed marriage, Alanzo feels rejected.

Dae is Buddhist and Alanzo is Catholic. Because of their love for one another, they have shared to some extent in each other's religious practice, but each of them is deeply committed to his own religion. Early in their relationship Alanzo said, "Dae, I'm gonna make you a Catholic one day." Dae has never forgotten that. Alanzo has also told Dae-Ho how grateful he is for being introduced to Buddhism but Dae has not really believed this. Alanzo has not suggested it, but Dae-Ho fears that if they get married, Alanzo will want a Christian wedding ceremony; Dae would want a ceremony that reflects both of them spiritually.

Alanzo can be very aggressive and speaks quickly. Dae-Ho feels that he lets Alanzo have most of what he wants in their relationship—the house they live in, how they spend most of their holidays, where they vacation, the design of their rings, and so on. But for the most part, it has worked well for both of them. When Dae is adamant about what he wants, Alanzo usually yields to him because it is important to him for Dae to be happy. All in all, they are a great team together.

After two years of feeling rejected by Dae about marriage, Alanzo began to be even more assertive in making decisions not relating to marriage. A few weeks before Easter, Alanzo told Dae that he arranged for them to visit his family for Easter weekend. Dae told Alanzo that there was no way he was going, and that Alanzo had no right to make those plans without discussing this with him. Dae said, "You're not going to make me a Christian. And I don't want to be with your stinking family." Alanzo didn't know what Dae was talking about regarding being a Christian, but he was angry and hurt because it was yet another time he felt rejected. Before he realized what he was doing, Alanzo shoved Dae hard. Dae-Ho fell down, hit his head and suffered a concussion. Dae told Alanzo that he was glad that they had not gotten married. Heart-broken, Alanzo does not respond.

Reflection on Story. Right now, both Dae-Ho and Alanzo are grieving deeply. In addition to the love they have for one another, the relationship has very specific meanings and values attached to it for each of them.

Dae-Ho's Values. First, Dae-Ho greatly values his relationship with his parents, as much if not more than his relationship with Alanzo. For the first seven years that Dae-Ho and Alanzo have been together, Dae-Ho hid his sexuality and his relationship with Alanzo from his parents. When he told his parents about his and Alanzo's relationship, his parents insisted that only because of his Americanization he is in relationship with a man. Dae has explained to his parents that he knew when he was a little boy in Korea that he was gay. But they refuse to hear him. As much as Dae-Ho loves Alanzo, he does not feel that he could break his parents' honor and their hearts and marry a man, especially a man who is neither Korean nor Buddhist. He knows that his parents would not come to the wedding ceremony, and that would break his heart. Now, he is also anxious about how to explain to his parents how he got hurt at home.

Second, Dae-Ho values the sense of safety he has had with Alanzo. Because of Alanzo's assertiveness and strength, Dae-Ho felt very safe. With this recent incident, now he no longer does. As he is recuperating from his concussion, he fears that it would be foolish of him to take the risk of marrying someone who has just pushed him down wondering if it is likely to escalate to more abuse. It pains Dae to think that he will also lose the home that he has made together with Alanzo, yet the idea of being at home with Alanzo does not feel safe anymore. Dae also thinks that Alanzo never considers what Dae wants when making decisions. He also is angry at himself for being too weak and giving in to Alanzo too often.

Third, Dae-Ho values his connection to Buddhism. He is convinced that Alanzo was serious when he made the comment about Dae becoming Catholic, and that Alanzo didn't mean it when he told Dae how much he appreciates Buddhism.

Alanzo's Values. First, he is grieving the loss of the longing he has had all of his life to be happily married—legally, emotionally, and spiritually.

Before he hurt Dae, he kept hoping it would happen one day, and now he is convinced that it never will. Alanzo has always wanted to be in a loving marriage like his parents. When he was 24, even though he knew that he was gay, Alanzo married a woman and hoped that he could be satisfied. After being married with his wife for five years and having two children with her, he knew that he could not continue the lie anymore. He became depressed for the lie that he felt he was living. It took everything he had within him to tell his wife the truth and to ask for a divorce. When he told his parents about his sexuality, they told him that he was going to hell. Alanzo has never believed that God doesn't love him just as he is and he really wants a public religious blessing honoring his and Dae-Ho's love.

Second, Alanzo greatly values the sense of safety he has had with Dae-Ho. Dae has been his rock. When he met Dae-Ho, Alanzo felt that all the pain he went through before was worth it to finally be with the love of his life. It took so many years for him to connect with someone as wonderful as Dae-Ho and he can't imagine being with anyone else. Now that he is 53 years old, Alanzo fears that he will live the rest of his life alone.

Third, Alanzo is also grieving that he is not the person that he thought himself to be. His self-image has been shattered. He never imagined himself hurting Dae or anyone. Now, he is angry at himself for causing Dae-Ho to be hurt.

Some things Alanzo and Dae-Ho knew about their values before, and some were revealed more clearly to them only during their pain and grief. Each of them will interpret the experience for themselves based on both their own values and approaches to life. Will they allow the experiences to prompt them to talk with each other more openly about what they are grieving, and to share the fears and anxieties that each of them has had for years? Will they retreat into silence and run away from each other in an attempt to get away from the pain? Will they allow themselves to explore what helps each of them to feel safe, loved and respected? Will they use the experience to talk more deeply about what their respective values about marriage and family?

Like Alanzo and Dae-Ho, when you have experienced love-hurt, you are suddenly hurled into a universe of grieving. How you grieve depends upon the meaning and value you have attached to what you have lost. Sometimes you may not know how much you value certain people or things until you lose them. You can use the pain of your grieving to help you learn more about your needs, values, and wants. You can use your grieving to help you gain more clarity about your overall approach life and the attachments that you may have that you rely upon to get through life. How you interpret your experiences in the world greatly influences your ability to move through your grieving brought on by love-hurt. See Chapter 1 "Why Do You Hurt Me" to examine attachments you may have that help you feel safe or special in the world. And see Chapter 6 "How Do I Take Care of Myself?" for some useful tools for self-care in the midst of your grieving.

Ask Angels and Ancestors for Help

My mother's death occurred just as I was finishing my doctoral dissertation to submit for my dissertation defense. Because I was grieving, I had no energy to finish the last of what I needed to do. Also because of my grieving, I didn't care whether or not I completed the Ph.D. degree I had invested eight years of my life pursuing. I was having trouble focusing and writing. So I called for the help of the angels and ancestors, and help they did. When I defended my dissertation the next month, my committee expressed their surprise at how much I was able to accomplish, especially given my mother's death. I know that I did not do it alone.

Often when you are hurting, you may become inclined to feel that you should be able to go on with business as usual or think that you don't want to burden anyone with your heavy stuff. You do not need to bear the burden of your pain all by yourself. There are people in your life as well as angels and ancestors who are available to help you. Both angels and ancestors are spirits that will whisper words of empowerment and comfort, words of correction and protection. When you are clear about which direction and steps you are ready to take into greater wholeness, ancestors and angels will support you in making those steps.

You are not alone. As you feel like you are all alone, driving uphill, carrying a heavy load on a slippery road at night, remember that angels and ancestors are with you to support and guide you. Don't be afraid to reach out to them. Perhaps you have heard a whisper or received some kind of instinctual nudge prompting you to turn a particular corner and there you met a friend or stranger who brightened your day. Or perhaps just when you needed someone to talk with, a friend calls saying, "Something told me to call you." These are signs of the presence and support of angels and ancestors. They are here for you, reach out and take advantage of their wisdom and nurture just for you.

Because life doesn't stop while you are grieving from relationship hurts, see the list below for a list of strategies to help you balance your grieving with your ongoing living. These strategies will help sustain you in light of the wearying and disorienting effects of grieving.

1. No self-judgment or self-flagellation.
   a. Remind yourself that grieving is not a sign of weakness, but a sign that the way of relating that you have valued has ended.
   b. Remind yourself that it's okay to cry. It will help release the pain.
   c. Know that "You grieve the way you live." Observe yourself and gain insight about you.
   d. Extend grace to yourself—there will be up days and down days.
2. Breathe deeply. Deep breathing increases the flow of oxygen to your brain and other organs, improving your thinking and overall functioning.
3. Set aside a ritual space and time to be/talk with Spirit and gain insights about what happened and how to move forward.
4. Let yourself rest, including between meetings and activities.
5. Create and use a wholeness network—
   a. Support persons to do what you don't have energy to do for yourself, such as praying, scheduling structured activities (especially for evenings, weekends and holidays), reminding you to pay bills, opening mail, and preparing meals.
   b. Support groups facilitated by a counseling professional.
   c. Medical and mental health care providers.
   d. Holistic health treatments, such as, herbal supplements, medications, massage, acupuncture, Reiki, energy work, and aromatherapy.
6. Move your body as much as you can—exercise, walking, yoga.
7. Connect with the art within you and others—music, painting, poetry, etc.
8. Surround yourself with positive thinking people, loving animals, & living plants.
9. Plan twice as much time to complete your usual tasks.
10. Plan one task each day and complete it.

11. Keep major decision-making to a minimum.
12. Talk to God often and in whatever ways you need. You don't have to protect God's feelings; say whatever is on your heart.
13. Remind yourself it's not dishonoring anyone if you laugh even while you grieve.
14. Establish a regular routine that supports the level of energy you have now.
15. Plan ahead for the "firsts"—first holiday and other events reminding you of how life has been or you hoped it to be before the hurt.

The Pain Is All I Have

A second challenge to letting go of our love-hurt is the relationship we can form with our pain.

As suggested in the song, "Good Morning Heartache," sometimes it feels that pain is all there is left of the relationship that ended. In a way, pain can give you a sense of still being connected with the person who has left you. When you feel dead inside, pain might be the only thing that helps you know you are still alive. Or when you have been hurting for a long while, there comes a point where you can't even imagine your life without pain because your identity can become connected with your pain. Your love-hurt can become your companion.

A tremendous opportunity you have as you experience love-hurt is to accept the reality of what has happened and how that has changed your life, without accepting the pain from the loss as an inevitable part of your new reality. Yes, you are forever changed by the hurts you experience, but you also get to determine what those changes are within you based on the approach you bring to the experience, how you interpret the experience, and how you use the experience to write the next chapter of your life.

The following story provides an example of what it can look like when you cling to a relationship that is over.

> When Connie and Joel's relationship ended, it was difficult for both of them, because they really loved each other. While they were together as a couple, despite their love for one another, because of Joel's unhealed wounds, he kept becoming involved with other women. Although he repeatedly contested, "We're just friends," Connie knew that something romantic was going

on with Joel and his "friends." Connie decided to herself, "Two can play at this game. I'll show you how it feels, and see if you like it." When Connie got involved with another man, she was drawn in by how much he adored her and decided to end things with Joel. When she did that, because Joel never liked to be alone, he hooked up with one of the women he was seeing. Even though Connie was in a relationship with another man, she was still in love with Joel. When it appeared to Connie that Joel had moved on with his life, and didn't seem to miss her, it seemed her as if their six years together were canceled out. She became furious.

One day, she and her new man arrived unannounced and uninvited to Joel's home that he shared with his new woman. Connie and her new guy were accusing Joel of something that he had not done. Connie's new man was ready to defend his woman. Joel tried to explain that there must have been some misunderstanding, and that he meant no harm to Connie at all. He pulled Connie over to the side to speak privately and asked her what this was all about, and how could they fix it. She replied, "How could you just move on like we never happened? If pain is the only way you remember what we had, then I'll help you remember."

Reflection on Story. For Connie, the pain was all that she had left of a relationship that had been special to her. She had never loved anyone at that point in her life like she loved Joel. They had a magic together. Her pain kept that magic alive and kept her feeling connected with Joel. Yet, as long as she was clinging to her pain, she could not let go of the relationship nor open herself to new rich possibilities of love.

Clinging to the past is more likely to occur when you fear an uncertain future or when your sense of what helps you to feel safe or special is attached to someone or something that has ended.

Forgiveness at the Threshold of Wholeness

The third challenge to healing love-hurt is that a lack of forgiveness keeps us trapped in the pain. Trapped by our own self-protections.

Eighteenth-century English poet Alexander Pope said, "To err is human; to forgive, divine," pointing us to the spiritual significance of forgiveness. To engage in forgiveness is to use it as a spiritual resource for wholeness.

When you don't forgive others for their hurtful actions toward you, you remain tightly bound to them and their emotional pain. Remember that hurt people hurt others. As long as you are bound to them, you cannot heal your pain. And when you don't forgive yourself for what you've done, because you are holding onto the belief that you deserve to hurt for the pain you caused someone else, you will be stuck in the pain.

Across centuries, religions and academic disciplines, there has been a lot written about forgiveness—what it is, its value to individuals and communities, and how to extend it or receive it.

For example, in the 12th century, Torah scholar and physician Moses Maimonides wrote his definitions and requirements of forgiveness in a code of Jewish law.[10] For Maimonides, forgiveness is about teshuvah, a process by which a transgressor is "returned" to their connection with the community in ways that foster wholeness for the community and the transgressor. While the process of teshuvah is designed to return an individual and a community to wholeness, because wholeness is ultimately a spiritual state of being, even these steps cannot determine to what extent someone is spiritually whole.

Many of us believe that forgiveness is important, yet find it hard to do. While we may extend compassion and help someone who has hurt us, we are still often inclined to withhold forgiveness.[11]

Research studies on the issue of forgiveness show that over 90 percent of us believe that forgiveness is important to give to others, yet less than 45 percent of us report actually forgiving someone who has hurt us. I don't believe that this is because we're all just a bunch of hypocrites, but because of how we define forgiveness and because we haven't been given straightforward tips for how to do it.

How do you define forgiveness? Does your definition of forgiveness offer any strategies for your wholeness?

In a study examining the connection between forgiveness and emotional healing, psychologists Mark Rye and Kenneth Pargament define forgiveness as "letting go of negative affect (e.g., hostility), negative cognition (thoughts of revenge), and negative behavior, (e.g., verbal aggression) in response to a considerable injustice, and also may involve responding positively toward the offender (e.g., compassion)."[12] In their definition, Rye and Pargament emphasize forgiveness as both letting go of negative feelings, thoughts, and behaviors as well as engaging in positive feelings, thoughts, and behaviors as a choice in response to a wrong. They say that this kind of letting go is what helps people to begin a process of emotional healing.

Many of us think of forgiveness as "letting someone off the hook." You might hear yourself say, "I'm not gonna give him the satisfaction." When you are attached to that as your goal, you're the one who ends up not having satisfaction in your life. You are the one that forgiveness really lets you off the hook of pain.

The process of forgiveness enables you to look honestly at your attachments and your ways of thinking. As you assess whether your thoughts and attachments are helping or hindering your healing, you can make conscious choices for your life. By making the choice to forgive, you begin a process of cutting your connection to the pain.

Forgiveness also empowers you to remember the hurtful experience in ways that enable you to learn, grow, and heal. Forgiveness enables you to recognize what you have come through and appreciate the new opportunities now present in your life that emerged from the hurtful situation. Forgiveness becomes possible as you let go of clinging to the way things have been and opening yourself to new transforming experiences.

If you think of your life as your story, every major experience marks a new chapter. You have the opportunity to choose which characters, places, themes or issues will carry into the next chapter, but choose you must. You are not passive in your own life's story. Even though both hurtful and pleasing actions may be directed towards you—actions over which you did not have control—you do have control over how you respond. It is your response to those experiences that writes your life story, chapter after chapter. But to write the next chapter, you must end the previous chapter in one way or other. Forgiveness is a vital tool for helping you to resolve the issues and themes in one or more chapters of your life to begin creating space for new ones.

Forgiveness of others and forgiveness of yourself are spiritually connected. As I shared in the Introduction to this book, I admit that I have hurt people that I love. Like the stories throughout this book, my hurtful actions were my knee-jerk reactions to feeling aggrieved in some way. What I discovered is that without forgiving myself I also held onto the pain of what was "done to me." As I understood that my hurtful actions were pointing out things for me to see about myself, I learned the need for me to forgive myself so that I could create a new love narrative and something new for my life story.

As I observed my patterns of when I hurt others it was most often connected with my own choice to subjugate my needs and desires, and put other people's needs and desires ahead of my own. When I felt "put on the back burner" for extended periods of time, I became resentful. I often put my needs and desires last, because the love narrative I had directed me that was what I was supposed to do. Then I realized about me that when I experienced resentfulness for a sustained period of time, I am likely to become critical and mean. Once I accepted that this is a part of my emotional fabric, I made different choices about how I show up in my relationships. Now, I pay more attention to my own needs to keep me emotionally healthy. Understanding this has helped me to forgive myself for how I have hurt others. And it has given me compassion toward others who have hurt me.

Each of us interprets and makes meaning of our experiences, both those in which we were the one hurt and where our actions were hurtful to someone else. As you interpret your experiences, you write your life story. When you know that your sense of safety is not contingent upon someone else, you can write your own story in ways that are life-giving for yourself. You have the choice power to write a new love narrative, one that will help you release your tight hold onto self-protection, grieve in ways that empower you, create a new identity for yourself that is not associated with the love-hurt, and yield to the divine impulse within you to forgive.

I've described what forgiveness is and some of its benefits, so how do you forgive?

The definition of forgiveness offered above by Rye and Pargament provides some useful guides for how to forgive others. Rye and Pargament define forgiveness as letting go of such things as hostility, thoughts of revenge, and aggressive words and extending compassion toward those who have hurt you. So how do you do that?

In Chapter 4 "What's Wrong with Me?" I listed some suggestions for how to forgive yourself that can be applied to forgiving others. Here's a shortened version of these strategies:

(1) Remember you can only do what you know how to do.
(2) Love and extend blessings to the little child within the person who hurt you.
(3) Speak affirming words to yourself about the person who hurt you.
(4) Remember that the hurt you experienced was your loved one's knee-jerk reaction to anxiety and fear.

(5) Shift your focus from what's been done to you to what is now possible for you.

(6) Know that the loved ones who hurt you are more than their mistakes.

(7) Ask for guidance from Spirit to strengthen your willingness to forgive.

Forgiveness is a healing salve for your love-hurts. Use it generously and open wide the portals of your heart to receive abundant wholeness and joy in your life.

Reflection Questions

1. In what ways do you self-protect and guard yourself from the potential of love-hurt? What strategies other than self-protection might help you feel safe to be vulnerable in your relationships?
2. What love narrative do you tell yourself about being hurt in love?
3. How would it add more peace in your life if you reach out more often to angels, ancestors, and others in your life for support?
4. In what ways are you grieving past hurts? How is your grieving impacting how you show up in your relationships now with family, friends, co-workers, fellow worshipers, strangers, and others?
5. To what extent are you clinging to your pain as your companion or as part of your self-identity?
6. Who do you need to forgive?

Chapter Eight

Why, Who and How Do I Trust Again?

What was it about relationships that made you feel so vulnerable?
Oh, right. A relationship. In any relationship, you put yourself
out there. You exposed all of your sensitive nerve endings and your
heart and you just had to hope that you trusted the right person.
—Courtney Cole

In a primal sense, safety, and specialness are about survival. When we have experienced love-hurt, unconsciously our fears caution us not to trust others again or we will cease to exist. Perhaps you have heard yourself say, "If this happens again, I won't be able to survive." The fear of not surviving can lock us in a prison of self-protection that keeps us from being fully alive. Trust is the key that unlocks that prison gate. But why should you trust again? How do you determine who to trust? How do you find the ways to trust when you've been so hurt?

The Value-Add to Your Life

Depending on our own personalities, backgrounds, and life experiences, we trust different people or things to help us feel safe and special.

Trust is having a strong reliance or firm confidence in the ability and character of someone or something to function as promised, now and in the future. It is a confidence that you can count on someone or something to show up consistently in ways that foster your sense of specialness and safety, and a faith that you won't be disappointed. Without trust, you cannot fully be free. For trust in someone or something beyond yourself strengthens your sense of safety to explore the world, take new risks, and expand beyond the limiting horizons of your comfort zone.

When you have been hurt, trust is a point of crisis. In Chinese, the word crisis is formed by two symbols

危機

which mean danger and opportunity. When you have experienced love-hurt, your tendency is to focus on the certain danger. You fear that danger is lying in wait to pounce on you when you least expect it, if you allow yourself to trust someone again. Self-protections that keep replaying images of past hurtful moments over and over make it more challenging for you to recognize or feel safe enough to see the opportunities for wholeness that are present in this new moment that has been made possible by the love-hurt experience.

Fragile trust combined with unhealed wounds make it more likely that you bring an even greater need for safety and specialness to your relationships and a lower tolerance for anything that appears to leave you feeling less safe or special. As the expression goes, "A burnt child dreads fire." When you have experienced the fires of love-hurt, the mere smell of smoke triggers you to self-protect.

At times in knee-jerk reaction to someone's thoughtless words or actions you may become triggered to self-protect. Sometimes, without knowing it, someone may hit into wounds that you don't even know that you have. Or someone may not affirm how special you are in the ways you want or need to be affirmed for it to count for you. Or someone may not help you feel safe in the ways you long for. The self-protective ways you react when not feeling safe or special enough can contribute to others not feeling safe or special. And so the cycle begins and often escalates. Without understanding how it all started, you can experience deep love-hurt and the trust in the relationship is greatly damaged or completely broken.

Opening yourself to trusting another human being is always a risk. You have the option of focusing on the potential dangers to love and "playing it safe" or emphasizing the potential opportunities to love and truly knowing you are safe in ways that are not dependent upon a particular person or set of circumstances.

Here is a story from my life that illustrates what can happen when you don't allow yourself to trust again.

> When I met Jeanette and Steve, they had been married for several years. Both of them had been married before. Steve was passionate in his love for his wife. I could tell that Jeannette loved Steve very much too, but she was guarded. At first, I thought it was just that she was more reserved in her style than he, and then I realized that she was protecting herself from being hurt. I sensed that she was not protecting herself from Steve but from lingering memories of pains from her past.
>
> When Jeanette was diagnosed with a life-threatening illness, I visited her in the hospital and asked her to tell me more about her life, especially her previous marriages. As she told me a little about each one, I could hear the pain in her voice and see how tightly she held her body. Then I said to her, "Love like you've never been hurt." She groaned loudly, and sat silent for a long while. Then she told me more about the love-hurts she had experienced before she met Steve. She realized that she had not fully allowed herself to relax in Steve's love for her. We talked about how different Steve has demonstrated himself to be from her previous husbands. That day, she decided to open herself more fully to Steve than she ever had before. During the last few months of Jeannette's life, I saw her really let Steve's love in and saw her love him without holding back any aspects of herself. I know that it made their final months together more healing, intimate and precious for both of them.

Reflection on Story. Prior to my conversation with Jeannette, she and Steve had a good relationship. Yet I often imagine how much more joy-filled, love-filled, and free it could have been if she had been able to trust more throughout their marriage. Trusting more in Steve's love, Jeannette might have healed from the hurts she endured from her earlier marriages instead of only lessening the pain as scar tissue formed over the wounded places in her heart. So often, because we are afraid to trust again our pain remains unhealed and we miss out on deeper, richer, and fuller intimacies with others and greater freedom within ourselves.

What helped Jeannette take the risk of opening herself more fully to trust again? I believe that because she was seriously ill she felt that she didn't have anything to lose and she was willing to take the risk. She was in a deeper space of trust in her life, as she was relying in and trusting in Divine Spirit with her health and all aspects of her life perhaps more deeply than she had in a long time. When she was hurt each time before, even though she continued to love God, there was a part of her that had become somewhat guarded with God too.

When you are reticent to trust in Spirit, it leaves you feeling less safe and less special in the world. You can confuse the resources in your life with the Source of your life to help you feel safe and special in the world. Those resources, however, are likely to be imperfect, uncertain, and changing. Because those who love you best will at times unintentionally hit into the tender, unhealed places in your hearts, even they may hurt you. In whom do trust you then?

In Whom Do You Trust?

When your trust in others becomes greater than your trust in Spirit, you are not likely to feel secure regardless of the measures you may take to feel safe or special. As a consequence, your capacity to trust other human beings becomes more fragile and your anxiety high.

For several years, Sandy, a few other colleagues, and I led an interspiritual support group for women survivors of sexual abuse, called Taking Back My Life. Much of the effectiveness of the group stemmed from how we invited women to raise the question that they had not felt safe enough to ask before, "Where was God when I was being abused?" For many of the participants to have the space to explore this question began a process of much-needed healing in their relationships with the Divine.

Having the safe space to express their questions, anger, and doubts about God enabled them also to reflect on the ways that they have felt held and strengthened by God. Being able to question helped them to look at their experiences more holistically. Like many of us who have been hurt, women participating in Taking Back My Life were so gripped by their hurts and pains that they had not been able to see as clearly the ways in which they had also grown into more compassionate, strong, creative, and thoughtful human beings stemming from their hurtful situations. Exploring these issues helped them redefine what supported them in feeling safe and special. It deepened their trust in God, as the first one to trust. This shifted how they trusted other people, with less need for others to be perfect and greater reliance that they would be well even if they are hurt again. Trusting God more strengthened many of the women to take the risks of love again. Deepening their trust in Spirit brought greater balance and lessened their emotional pendulum swing from high self-protection to high fantasy thinking about the role of relationships in their lives.

Ultimately, taking the risk of trusting again helps us to remember and connect with the truth that there is more love in the world than there is hurt. It is a truth that we most easily observe in times of natural disasters and crises when people liberally pour out care and compassion to loved ones and strangers alike. If we allow ourselves to be open to and trust in love, love has a greater and stronger voice within our hearts and minds than hurt and pain. There really are more opportunities in love than there are dangers. You get to make the choice which you will focus on more. Whatever you focus your thoughts on you manifest more of in your life.

Chambers of Love

The capacity and longing to trust is part of our human nature. When we have been pained by love-hurt, we often transfer our trust from people to other attachments in our lives, such as coping strategies, persona/ social image, self-image, beliefs, traditions and beliefs, and worldviews. Which of these attachments we are more likely to rely upon to feel safe may be influenced by significant messages we received—directly and indirectly—from our families, teachers, religious leaders, peers, and media. People and things that were absent in our formative years can also contribute to what we long for to help us feel safe and special, believing "Everything would be okay if I had _____."

But how do you know who is healthy and appropriate for you to trust, especially while you are still healing from love-hurt? The design of the ancient Jewish temple, with its intentional system of preparation and eligibility for entrance into its distinctive courts, serves as a useful metaphor to explore this important question. Intentional thought about who you trust to have what kind of access to your being can be a valuable tool to enhance not only your sense of safety and specialness in the world, but your overall wellbeing and wholeness.

In a letter to the church at Corinth, Apostle Paul wrote, "Do you not know that your bodies are temples of the Holy Spirit who is in you?"

(1 Corinthians 6:19, Holy Bible). Consider yourself—mind, body, and spirit—as a temple consisting of seven distinctive chambers.

The Temple of Your Being

Discerning Who to Trust and with What

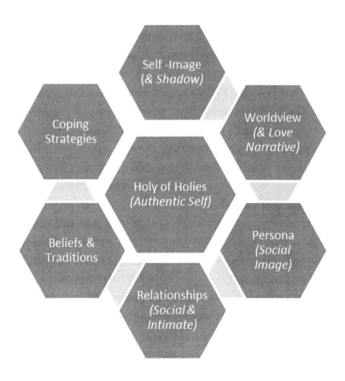

Persona—Outermost Chamber Accessible to Everyone
Access to Other Chambers Based on Preparation & Eligibility
Holy of Holies—Most Selective Chamber

Instead of having an either-or approach to trust—either you trust or you don't—regard trust as a muscle that you build incrementally as you allow people access to who you are, one emotional room at a time.

The initial chamber of your persona serves as an intermediary space between your public self and the more intimate and sacred spaces of your being. The space is accessible to everyone. Here is where you begin to learn some things about yourself and others, the things on your surface.

The kinds of resources present in the persona chamber (social status, reputation, material possessions, financial wealth), as well as the rooms of your coping strategies, religious beliefs, worldviews and so on, that support your sense of safety and specialness, can easily become emotional attachments. The emotional anchors that are present in the public spaces of your being are more easily acquirable. Yet, because these things are often fleeting and dependent upon how other people perceive you, the fear of losing the people and things in your outer chambers can leave you feeling tremendous anxiety.

Depending upon your past experiences and your love narrative, there are two likely reactions to this feeling of anxiety shaping how and who you trust. First, you might maintain such a high degree of distrust and self-protection that you don't allow anyone into your inner courts, including those individuals who could support your emotional health and spiritual wholeness best. A second response, that is a polar opposite, is that you might move people into your inner spaces too quickly for fear that if you don't they will leave you. This response makes it more likely that you will experience love-hurt because you have not gleaned enough information to assess the person's emotional readiness to be in your most intimate space. The longer-term consequence of this is that you become more inclined to keep everyone in your outer emotional spaces, perhaps including yourself.

Each of us relies more in certain emotional courts than others to assess who and what we use as anchors in our lives. Perhaps if you grew up poor or grew up perceiving that you had to be perfect to be loved, the chamber of the persona, where material wealth and social status are emphasized, may be the court you rely upon most for your sense of safety and specialness. Starting there as you meet people may be appropriate to assess if there is more to the relationship that might be possible. To stay there, however, will leave you feeling unsatisfied. More money, power and influence, a bigger house, a more prestigious position, and your children in "right" the schools cannot foster a sense of wellbeing, of feeling totally safe or unconditionally special in the world. Neither these things nor the people with whom these are the only things that you share can foster this wellbeing because they are conditional and fleeting. These "courtships" lack emotional depth.

Before Entering Your Holy Space

Ensure that in your court of relationships that you have a few rooms. The purpose of these rooms is to provide you with emotional spaces to prepare for different kinds and levels of relationships. It is space for you to assess who has the qualities that you need to support you in your exploration and discovery of your authentic self, your holy of holies. It also provides a space for others to prepare themselves to be ready for a more intimate relationship with you. It's like having a "mud room" in your emotional home where you and others can take off some of the gook from previous relationships before entering your sacred space.

Before inviting anyone into your inner emotional courts, make sure you observe them and learn about them in all of your outer chambers first. When you are assessing who to let in your inner space, one court at a time, consider these few things about yourself and about the other person.

Things about You	*Things about the Other Person*
▪ The goals that I have for my life—emotionally, spiritually, socially, professionally, financially & so on	▪ The goals he has for his life—assess whether compatible, complementary with mine
▪ Unhealed emotional wounds that I have that impact how I show up in relationships	▪ How self-aware she is about her unhealed wounds
▪ My patterns of letting people in too fast or keeping people out too long	▪ What he has expressed about his relationship patterns
▪ The things I have learned about myself as I have related with him in my outer courts	▪ Things you are learning about her as you relate in various outer courts

▪ When I am ready to invite her into one of my inner chambers, the first and safest one should be _____	▪ The extent to which his approach and pace to becoming more intimate that matches with mine
▪ The ways I am ready to heal and the supports I need to heal	▪ What she expressed being ready to heal and the support she needs
▪ What I have to offer him to support his healing and learning that also supports my healing and learning	▪ What does he offer to support my healing and learning that also support his healing and learning
▪ I access emotional and spiritual supports on a regular basis to help me connect with her (resource) yet not becoming attached (source)	▪ She accesses her emotional and spiritual supports regularly and safeguards against codependence

If the other person you are reflecting about is someone who has hurt you in the past, here are some additional things to consider:

- What indicators are there that he acknowledges that his actions hurt you, and how?
- To what extent does she desire to make amends and make changes in her way of relating with you?
- What indicators there are that he understands what triggered him to behave in ways that were hurtful to you?
- To what extent can she hear you talk about your pain and not try to justify or defend her actions?
- How much is he willing and able to take it slowly to rebuild the trust that he damaged?
- What indicators are there that she has the emotional maturity to facilitate and trust in the process of reconciliation?

When you feel vulnerable and exposed to someone who knows you well and who has hurt you, if after reflecting on questions above, and you want to maintain the relationship and rebuild the trust, take your time. You may have the tendency to rush back into the relationship that you have known. Slow down, and allow yourself time to get clear about what new boundaries you need as you move toward reconciliation. Perhaps the person who hurt you is not ready or mature enough for the degree of emotional connection that you seek. If that is the case, you can begin to discern about what kind of relationship makes best sense for both of you given who you are and where you are in your respective spiritual journeys. Intentional time to discern—listen to your heart—to know what is best for you in this moment. Next month or next year you might be able to see things differently. So remind yourself that if it's in your spirit's best interest for you and the person who hurt you to continue in relationship together in some way or other, all will be well. Be open to the possibility that it might be in your spirit's best interest—for your healing, learning, and growing—for the relationship to change from what it has been, or perhaps for it to end. Let go of the process and the outcome. As you do, you will have incredible peace and feel the burden of the pain begin to lift from your heart.

None of these ideas for your reflections are perfect for every situation but definitely can assist you in determining how to move forward into greater trust. Not merely for you to feel safe and special, but to know that you are.

As 14th century mystic Julian of Norwich said, "All is well, all shall be well, and all manner of things shall be well." The more you trust in this truth, the more you will be able relax in your relationships and to see others and yourself clearly without the distorting filter of the fear that you won't be safe and special. Listen deeply within your heart.

Get Ready, Get Set, Trust!

Two important steps that can prepare you to trust again are 1) reflecting on the things that have challenged you in trusting, and 2) exploring some tools for discerning (listening with your heart) about whom to trust. But of course, there's nothing like actually trusting again. Trust is one of those spiritual paradoxes: the more you use it, the more of it you have. And the less you use it, the less of it you have.

In each moment, including this one, you have the opportunity to open yourself to be transformed by love. Trust is the key that enables you to unlock the prison of self-protection and empowers you step through the doorway into new and deeper experiences of love. Opening yourself fully to love transforms you. Focusing on the ways that trusting the right people, guided by Spirit, can strengthen your confidence to actually take the risks of trust and love again. Here's an example of the transforming power of trusting again someone who has hurt you.

Maria had decided not to trust her daughter Nicole ever again. Nicole had broken her heart too many times because of her drug addiction. Nicole has gone into treatment programs so many times that Maria has lost count. For the past five years Maria has been the legal guardian of Nicole's son, Michael. To protect him from the craziness that Nicole brings, three years ago, she got a restraining order to stop Nicole from coming to her home anymore.

Over a year ago, Nicole was hit and almost killed by a car as she was walking across the street, stoned. She had resigned herself the possibility of dying from drugs, but when her body was flying through the air after the SUV hit her, something really scared her. When she was lying in the hospital after the accident, she made a commitment to herself, her mother, her son, and God that if she lived, she would really become drug free. Maria has heard that promise from Nicole so many times that she no longer lets herself believe her because it hurts too much to live with the pain of constant disappointment.

After she was released from the hospital, Nicole went to a drug treatment center. This was her fourth time going through treatment. This time, for the first time, she honestly looked at the pain that she had been attempting to cover and medicate through drugs. She remembered how traumatized she was at age 14 when she discovered her father's body after he hanged himself. She remembered how emotionally unavailable her mother was for the first few years after her father's death. Nicole finally got in touch with how angry she was at her father for killing himself, angry at her mother for not having done something to prevent his suicide, and angry at her mother for not being able to support her when she needed her most. Once she got in touch with her anger, then she was able to realize and appreciate all that her mother has done for her through the years, including taking care of Michael.

Nicole completed her treatment program almost one year ago, and she has stayed clean and sober for the first time in 15 years. She has a job and started taking a couple of classes a community college. While Maria is glad to see the incredible progress that her daughter has made and is so proud of her, Maria is scared to trust her again. She is afraid that Nicole will break her and Michael's hearts again. As he watches his grandmother not trust his mother, Michael is wondering if he should protect himself from being hurt too. He really wants to have a relationship with his mother, but his grandmother keeps saying, "I'm not saying don't see your mother. Just be careful." One day after she said that, Maria saw a deep pleading in his eyes. Then she began asking herself how much longer she was going to distrust her daughter and what effect was that having on her grandson.

Maria thought about everything that she has seen Nicole do and say that is very different from before. In so many ways Maria feels she has her daughter back, the daughter before drugs, yet also more mature, much wiser, and more compassionate. When she thought about what she has seen in Nicole, she admitted to herself that really likes the woman Nicole has become. As they began to rebuild their relationship, Nicole shared with Maria that it wasn't until she got in touch with her anger that she could become drug-free. Nicole has encouraged that she, her mother and son go to therapy together to help them talk openly and honestly about whatever feelings they have had so that they can begin to heal. After resisting for a long while, Maria finally has agreed.

Reflection on Story. Understandably, it took a while for Maria to stop protecting herself from the pain she had experienced for so long. Because of the pain from her husband's suicide, she had built up thick, tall protective walls. When her daughter became addicted to drugs, Maria blamed herself, and reacting to the pain of that thought, she projected her anger onto her daughter. She made Nicole the sole reason for any unhappiness in her life rather than dealing with her own feelings. Maria used her daughter's addiction to drugs and all of the drama that came with that as an excuse not to look at her own pain. Once Nicole became clean and sober, Maria didn't have anyone else to blame or be angry at anymore. All she was left with was her own pain. Inspired by her grandson, Maria is ready to trust again.

Trusting again after deep love-hurt is indeed a point of crisis. It brings both danger and opportunity. It can be so scary because it opens you up to the possibility of being hurt again. It is also scary because trusting others, invites you into a deeper, more intimate, and more honest relationship with yourself. Instead of seeing yourself through the veil of what is wrong in other people's lives, trust invites you to enter into the holiest parts of yourself and to see your authentic self. This is a place of holiness and wholeness. Here, you know that you are safe and special.

When you truly know within your own holy of holies that you are safe and special, you can love and live like you've never been hurt. Because within your holy of holies, you can see yourself and others more clearly. As you see more clearly, you love more openly, compassionately, and wisely. The title song of the Broadway musical, On a Clear Day by Burton Lane, sums it well—

> *On a clear day, rise and look around you, and you'll see who you are.*
> *On a clear day, How it will astound you, That the glow of your*
> *being outshines ev'ry star.*
> *You'll feel part of ev'ry mountain sea and shore.*
> *You can hear, from far and near, A world you've never heard before.*
> *And on a clear day, On that clear day,*
> *You can see forever and ever more!*

With each step into your wholeness, may you see more clearly, trust more wisely, forgive more freely, and love more openly—forever more, like you've never been hurt. And with each new experience that lies ahead may you know more fully that you are safe, that you are special, and that you are loved.

Reflection Questions

1. In what ways do you self-protect when your spirit is inviting you to go deeper in your experiences of trust?

2. What do you do, upon whom do you trust and rely in those moments when both you and your loved one are caught in a loop of not feeling special or safe?
3. Which attachments do you use to help you feel special and safe that may be impeding you from more intimate and satisfying relationships?
4. What are you afraid you might uncover about yourself as you open yourself to trust others more?
5. How do you assess who is prepared and ready to enter the inner chambers of your emotional self?

Afterword

*We were born to manifest the glory of God that is within us. As
we let our own light shine, we unconsciously give other people
permission to do the same. As we are liberated from our own fear,
our presence automatically liberates others.*
—Marianne Williamson

So what difference does loving like you've never been hurt really make
as your life is turned right-side-up? There are some tremendous benefits
that I've experienced in my life and observed in the lives of others that I
hope will inspire you to practice loving in this new way. I say "new way"
because most of us have learned to fight, flee or emotionally freeze after we
have experienced love-hurt.

Like learning anything new—such as, driving a car, cooking a new
specialty meal, speaking a new foreign language—at the outset, loving like
you've never been hurt takes intentional focus and practice. When I get
hurt or scared, I still have to be intentional about making the choice to
love in ways that are not guided by fear and anxiety, but love and trust. The
more often I practice this kind of love it has become easier to do and feels
more natural each time I do it.

What helps me to continue to practice loving in this way is the vision I
have for what I want my life to look like and who I seek to be. As I practice
loving unconditionally and with healthy boundaries, my life is becoming
what my vision of living is. You can have the life you long for as you let go
of self-protections and your fight, flight, and freeze responses to love-hurts.
Here are some of the benefits.

1. **Freedom**. I could not have imagined how much freer I would feel
   when I let go of my anger and hurt. If I could have imagined it,

I would have done it l-o-n-g time before I actually did. I didn't realize how much I had become attached to certain resources in my life, and how much I limited the choices I made in order to ensure that those people and things would be there to "make" me safe and special. Loving like you've never been hurts enables you to appreciate the resources in your life without becoming attached to them to feel safe and special because this kind of love connects you with a deep inner knowing that you are safe. Instead of making choices guided by the fear of loss, you can choose to be guided by love. Loving like you've never been hurts helps you to know that your life is more than the sum of your attachments. Love helps you to know that you are really bigger than what your attachments and comfort zones can offer. Love expands you. As Jesus said to spiritual seekers, "You shall know the truth"—that you are wonderful, amazing, special, and that you are safe—"and the truth will set you free." Choices guided by love will set you free.

2. *Happiness.* Allowing yourself to be truly intimate with others increases the delight and joy you experience in life. Love and intimacy release the endorphins that intensify feelings of happiness. Love lifts you. If you grew up in a family in which unhappiness and dissatisfaction were the norm, it might be hard to imagine anything else as possible for your life. Perhaps you were taught to let love-hurts eclipse the wondrousness of love that is also present. Or perhaps you hesitate to strive for a more satisfying life for fear that you do not have "what it takes" to be happier, and "you can't teach an old dog new tricks." Maybe you're afraid that if you let yourself choose to be happy, you'll be devastated if it doesn't happen. I understand those fears. But the truth is happiness attracts happiness. Your free expression of happiness inspires others. Whether you are spending time with loved ones, working on your job, interacting with members of your religious group, or walking down the street, happiness shifts the atmosphere around you by tapping into whatever longings for happiness and joy there are within others. Instead of being a "player hater" who is envious of those who are happy, allow the happiness in others to stir up the happiness that is buried deeply within you. Although it may be covered up for safe-keeping, it's still in there. The more you feel their happiness, the greater yours increases as well.

3. ***Beauty and Miracles***. Albert Einstein says, "There are two ways to look at life. One is as though nothing is a miracle; the other is as though everything is." The more free and happy you are, the more you are able to perceive and appreciate beauty and miracles that are present every day. Barricading behind the walls of self-protection, defining your self-identity based on the love-hurts you've experienced, or clinging to the attachments of social image, coping strategies, and so on can block your ability to see the incredible wondrousness of the miracles and beauty in your life right now. Loving like you've never been hurt adjusts your perception to see beauty all around you and witness the miracles unfolding everyday. In the magnificence of trees as they go through various seasons of the year. In the miracle of life manifest in the giggles of little children as they explore the world and in the wrinkled faces of elders as they ponder new things they are learning. Loving like you've never been hurt sharpens your five natural senses and your sixth spiritual sense. Loving opens the eyes of your heart. Instead of the pain eclipsing the miracles, the miracles eclipse the pain. As you see beauty and witness miracles, your life is filled with abundant joy and peace.

4. ***Balance and Groundedness***. As you are able to recognize and celebrate the reality of beauty and miracles, you grow in your ability to be emotionally balanced and grounded. Yes, the ups and downs, the joys and sorrows of life continue to happen. When you are intentional about loving like you've never been hurt, the free flow of the love helps you not be knocked off balance as easily when love-hurts and other life challenges occur. Knowing that you are safe provides tremendous groundedness to be able to ride through the storms of life. Self-protections against hurt and attachments to resources that are uncertain ultimately cannot provide the deepest sense of safety. Only love can provide truest safety. Not love that is contingent upon what you get from someone else or dependent upon a person showing up in the ways that you want, but love that flows from within you unconditionally. Because you do not have control over what others say or do, reliance upon that does not foster your groundedness. Your groundedness and balance is "an inside job." Focus on the love within you and as you share this unconditionally, you will have emotional balance and be spiritually grounded.

5. ***Intimacy.*** I've heard people say that intimacy means "into me, see." When you've been hurt or when you don't feel good about yourself, the thought of being really seen can be both exhilarating and foreboding. The longing to be known and loved for who you are, and the fear of being exposed or rejected can be conflicting impulses within you that result in ambivalence and inconsistency in how you relate with others. Not allowing yourself to become intimate with people by using lots of sarcasm, being excessively overweight, working or volunteering so much that you don't have time for relationships, connecting with people primarily via internet social media, and so on are various strategies (conscious or unconscious) to keep people at a far-enough distance so that they won't be able to hurt you. These are strategies to keep people from getting too close and keep them locked out of the most sacred and tender parts of your heart. They can also keep you locked in loneliness. Loving like you've never been hurt allows you to unlock the fears that have been holding you hostage and enables you to envision and experience joys of being truly seen, known and loved. The prize of intimacy is freedom, a freedom greater than what can be experienced alone.

6. ***Authentic Self-Respect.*** When you've been hurt in love, the heightened sensitivities that form often can result in you "taking things personal," and being easily offended. You can presume that people are slighting you when they are not. If you have experienced people disrespecting you, especially during your childhood, you might not have a clear sense of how amazing and special you are and have limited self-respect. As Marianne Williamson writes, you "were born to manifest the glory of God that is within" you. Loving like you have never been hurt is the key to reconnecting with this spiritual truth about who you are. This love helps you to know the authentic you behind the masks of your social image and even truer than your self-image. Loving with the tenderness of a heart that has not been hurt enables you to go into the most sacred spaces within yourself with respect and reverence for the "holy of holies" within you. Self-love enables you to know that your authentic self is special and worthy to be loved and respected. Loving yourself like you've never been hurt gives you greater courage to be true to and nurture your authentic self, and to make decisions that honor who you truly are with dignity and grace. Being true "to thine

own self" enables you to tap into and draw deeply from the love, wisdom, and courage of Spirit within you.

7. ***Healthy Boundaries***. Hurt that is unhealed can lead you to be co-dependent, believing that your happiness is dependent on other people's happiness or to be less able to distinguish your needs and desires from someone else's. Loving like you've never been hurt helps you to see your inherent worth and value. As you do, you become more able to recognize that you deserve to be happy and that your happiness depends on the choices you make for your life and not on someone else's desires or actions. It helps you break the pattern of saying, "I'll decide when I see what he does." Loving like you've never been hurt fosters healthy boundaries that break through old patterns of codependence and blurred boundaries, and helps you create new norms of interdependence and mutuality. Loving like you've never been hurt may feel uncomfortable and strange at first, especially if you've been assigned a specific role in your family to put everyone's needs ahead of yours. But as you take time to get clear about what you want for your life and make choices that support your life goals, you will feel more empowered to honor all of who you are. As you do, you will attract people into your life who are also ready to be in mutually supportive relationships. Those already in your life may push against the new boundaries at first, but as you are consistent in honoring your own value and worth and in creating new boundaries for yourself, self-love like you've never been hurt will help you trust that whatever emerges in those relationships will be healthier and happier for you.

8. ***Trust Own Instincts***. Love-hurt, especially when others tell you what you are supposed to think or constantly tell you that they know better than you, can leave you questioning what you want and doubting your own instincts. Audre Lorde says, "If I didn't define myself for myself, I would be crunched into other people's fantasies for me and eaten alive." To live a life that is defined by other people's expectations, rulebooks, beliefs, and values can leave you feeling unfulfilled, depressed, low-energy, and empty. Following other people's definitions and labels about who you are, allowing others to control your choices, and deferring to what others say you need to do for your life does not nurture your authentic self. Loving like you've never been hurt helps you to tap into what your spirit knows and gives you the boldness to let your spirit guide

you into your truth. Define yourself for yourself. Everyday, practice trusting your own instincts, with little things and big. As you love you like this, you go deeply within your own spirit and connect to the wisdom within you and what fosters your wholeness and holiness. And your life is more fulfilling, fun and free.

9. ***Healthy Coping Behaviors***. As you stay in touch with love, and as you express gratitude for the capacity to love and be loved, the happier, freer, and more grounded you feel. Even when life challenges come, because you are more emotionally healthy and strong, you are more able to access healthy strategies to help you get through the challenges. Being emotionally and spiritually healthy gives you more strength to choose life and health rather than go to old default behaviors and patterns of coping that leave you feeling worse in the end. Being emotionally healthy helps you stay honest with yourself without shame or guilt as you consider or actually make unhealthy choices. When you don't beat up on yourself, but just look at your actions, you are more able to let go of the unhealthy coping strategies more quickly and return to what really helps you come back to your emotional balance. As you do, you can celebrate this as one of the miracles in your life.

10. ***Present Moment***. Love-hurts can leave you feeling fragmented across three dimensions of time. Part of you is in the past both reminiscing good times and attempting to figure out what you could have done to have avoided this pain. Part of you is in the future either foreshadowing the likelihood of more hurt or creating a fantasy of what you want your life to look like without any real basis to support it. Leaving only a part of you in the present moment. Going to the past or future is a way of running away from the pain of the present. Loving like you've never been hurt enables you to be present with what is and to see all of it clearly—not just the pain and danger, but also the opportunities and new possibilities wrapped up in the present. Being fragmented leaves you feeling broken and weak. Staying in the present moment gives you greater capacity for wholeness and strength. As you experience wholeness, you can think more clearly and perceive the options that are available to you.

11. ***Options***. When you've been hurt, and you're experiencing emotional concussion from being banged by pain, everything gets very cloudy and fuzzy for a while. In the midst of the fuzziness,

two things loom very large: the pain and the person who hurt you. Because these two things occupy so much emotional space, as you are attempting to make decisions about how to take care of yourself and how to move forward, it may seem that there are only one or two options available to you. You might hear yourself say, "Well, the only thing I can do is _____" or "She's left me no choice." Loving like you've never been hurt is like applying medicine that helps to reduce the emotional swelling that blocks your visibility so that you can see more of the options that are indeed available to you. Loving like you've never been hurt helps shrink the anxiety, blame, shame, and guilt that can blur and limit your vision. As you can see more clearly, you might even recognize the presence of some wondrous new options that had not been there before.

12. *Peace.* Holding tightly to your attachments that help give you a sense of safety and specialness leaves you feeling anxious. Loving like you've never been hurt reminds you that you are safe and you are special not based on these external attachments but because you are held in Love. Trust in the Universe. If you live your life as a believer in Murphy's Law that suggests that "what can wrong, will go wrong," then that's what you are likely to experience again and again. If, however, you imagine yourself being more satisfied with your life, you can begin to perceive the things and people who can best enhance your life and yet not become attached to them. Loving like you've never been hurt connects you with the reality that you are safe. Julian of Norwich says, "All is well. All shall be well. All manner of things shall be well." Love enables you to understand and embrace this truth no matter what may be happening in your life in any given moment. Loving like you've never been hurt reminds you that even in the stormiest rains and darkest nights, the sun is still shining. No matter what has happened, love is still the pathway to peace. Love helps you to hold onto that truth and to know that whatever challenges you may be experiencing in a moment, all is still well.

13. *Healing and Restoration.* During the course of your life, you experience many wounds—some intended, and most not. Focus on your love-hurts can lead you to identify yourself as wounded, broken and damaged. Your choices about relationships and how you live in the world can be shaped by a "damaged goods" identity. Loving like you've never been hurt transforms your identity from

broken to restored, from wounded to healed, from damaged to amazing. As you allow the prism love to be the lens through which you see yourself, you heal more and more, even the scar tissue. Love reduces your knee-jerk reactions when people come near the wounded areas and you become less likely to hurt others. As loving like you've never been hurt serves as a healing balm in your life, it also heals generational effects of love-hurts that have been passed to you, and you become free. This love even facilitates healing in your family.

14. *Hurts as Stepping Stones*. Abraham Lincoln said, "Most folks are about as happy as they make up their minds to be." The degree of satisfaction that you experience in your life reflects the choices you make about the thoughts you focus on, beliefs you hold, words you speak, and experiences that shape your life. Each time you experience hurts in your life, you choose how to perceive and how to relate with those hurts—guided by love or fear. If you truly want to be happy, choose to be guided by love. Loving like you've never been hurt helps you accept the reality of what has happened and how that has changed your life, without accepting the pain from the loss or the change as an inevitable part of your new reality. Yes, you are forever changed by the hurts you experience, but you also get to determine what those changes are within you based on the how you interpret the experience and how you use the experiences your journey. Loving like you've never been hurt gives you the vision for how to transform the stumbling blocks of hurts and pains that hinder your path into stepping stones that assist you along your life's journey.

15. *Clarity and Discernment*. A Course in Miracles tells us, "There is only love and fear." Fear, anxiety, and hurt create static that reduces your ability to hear things clearly and fog that impedes your ability to see well. In 1925, Gertrude Ederle, the first woman to attempt to swim the English Channel, was greatly impeded by fog. Because she couldn't see the shore, she gave into her weariness from swimming for hours through cold jelly-fish-filled waters, and climbed into the boat. Once she reached shore and realized how close she was, she said, "If I had only been able to see the shore, I could have made it." Loving like you've never been hurt greatly reduces the fog in your vision and static in your hearing so that you can see and hear more clearly. As your clarity increase, you are

able to discern what you need to do for you and how much farther you can go in your challenging situations. Clarity enables you to recognize early on when you are scared and how to move through your fears. Clarity enables you to make conscious choices about what people and things truly support you in having the life you want filled with joy and peace. Loving like you've never been hurt also equips you to see others more clearly in all the dimensions of who they are. As you discern the relative health of the people and situations in your life, you can make intentional and conscious choices about what promotes your highest good.

16. ***Emotional and Spiritual Maturity.*** Once, when I was hurt and angry, I said to a loved one, "You need to grow the hell up." While I was insightful in recognizing some potential growth opportunities for my loved one, I did not have the maturity to recognize that how I shared my insight was as important, if not more, than the insight itself. My hurtful knee-jerk commentary was really pointing out that I needed to grow up some more. Loving like you've never been hurt empowers you to minimize your knee-jerk responses by recognizing that even though feelings pop up, you still have control of how you respond to them and express them. Loving like you've never been hurt strengthens your ability to acknowledge earlier on what you need and the courage to give yourself what you need. It also enables you to draw upon your inner wisdom about who and how to invite into the various emotional courts of who you are—one court at a time. Loving like you've never been hurt helps you to grow up.

17. ***Physical Health.*** Love-hurts weaken your immune system. Loving like you've never been hurt strengthens your immune system. Love-hurts often lead you to neglect your self-care. Love reminds you that you deserve the best care from yourself and others. Loving like you've never been hurt is like a flu shot, immunization shots, vitamins and herbal supplements all rolled into one. As love increases your levels of peace and happiness, it releases the levels of serotonin and endorphins in your brain that help improve your health and happiness. As loving like you've never been hurt helps you to make wise choices about the coping strategies you use in times of stress, you are more able to maintain balance and calm in the midst of storms. Love promotes health.

18. *Financial Health*. Years ago, there was a reality TV show, "Do You Want to Be a Hilton?" that ended with a champagne toast to "the good life." So many of us focus on material possessions and financial wealth as the key to having a good life. Indeed these things can increase the comforts and conveniences in our lives. But as His Holiness the Dalai Lama says, "People must realize that even with all these comforts, all this money and a GNP that increases every year, they are still not happy." Sometimes, in the effort to fill emotional emptiness, you may seek to fill your life with a certain social image that social status, money and material possessions seem to satisfy. Yet when you rely on such material attachments to help you to feel happy, safe, and special, as you strive to have these things, you may be inclined to make some decisions that are not in your best financial interests. Loving like you've never been hurt brings you back to the truth that making financial choices guided by your attachments and anxieties can work against your goals of peace, safety, and happiness. Love empowers you to have material resources without becoming attached to them or defining yourself by them. Understanding that they are resources for your life but not the Source of your life. Loving like you've never been hurt connects you deeply to the Source.

19. *Inner Strength and Power*. Love-hurt leaves you feeling weak, and at times powerless. Loving like you've never been hurt is like connecting with a recharger battery. You have the power, given by the Spirit, to live a life that satisfies your spirit. Proclaim it loudly, "I got the power!" Love-hurt can leave you believing that your inner power is diminished and that if you use your limited power to make choices you know are right for you that you will not survive. You can become frozen in the ambivalence that fear brings. Audre Lorde says, "When I dare to be powerful—to use my strength in the service of my vision—then it becomes less and less important whether I am afraid." Loving like you've never been hurt reconnects you with the vision you have for your life. Love expands your vision and empowers and equips you to claim it with boldness and with joy.

20. *Compassion*. When you've been hurt, your focus is on finding ways to survive. Staying focused on your love-hurt can lead you to live in the world in ways that are often self-referential and narcissistic. While you may love others, your degree of empathy, caring and

compassion is limited because you live with the anxiety that you won't get your needs met. You fear that there won't be enough of whatever you are convinced that you need for you to survive, for you to be safe, and for you to feel special. Loving like you've never been hurt instills a great confidence within you that you will have all that you need to be well. This love helps you to know that God has already provided everything that you will ever need, even before the need presents itself. Loving and living with this confidence, your capacity for empathy and compassion expands beyond your wildest dreams. Loving like you've never been hurt helps you to heal the world just by being you.

I hope this list inspires you to know that loving like you've never been hurt is really worth it for you. Thank you for allowing me to travel "on the bus" with you (all ages of you) along your path into happiness and wholeness, your journey into joy and peace. Blessings on your journey.

Reflection Questions

1. How much do you really want the life you say you want?
2. Do you believe that you deserve the life you say you want? If not, what worldview and love narratives are you holding onto that are impeding you, and why?
3. What are you willing and ready to do differently to have the life you want?

Endnotes

1   Brennan, Cathy. "Emotional Vulnerability is an Act of Courage." *Inspired Soul Alliance*, March 7, 2012. http://www.inspiredsoulalliance.com/blog.

2   Jung, Carl G. *Man and His Symbols*. Translated by Marie-Luise von Franz. New York: Doubleday, 1964. Also see Jung, Carl. G. *The Archetypes and the Collective Unconscious*. Translated by R.F.C. Hull. New York: Bollingen Foundation, 1959.

3   Brown, Brené. *Daring Greatly*. New York: Gotham Books, 2012

4   Tillich, Paul. *Dynamics of Faith*. New York: Harper & Row, 1957, 44.

5   Jung, Carl Gustav. "Psychological Types," *Collected Works of C.G. Jung, Volume 6*. Princeton: Princeton University Press, 1971.

6   Deuteronomy 30: 15, 19,*Holy Bible*, NSRV.

7   Written by Irene Higginbotham, Ervin Drake, and Dan Fisher. Originally recorded by Billie Holiday on January 22, 1946 (Decca Records).

8   Kübler-Ross, Elisabeth. *On Death and Dying*. New York: Routledge, 1969.

9   Parkes, Colin Murray and Robert. S. Weiss. *Recovery from Bereavement*. New York: Basic Books, 1983.

10 See Everett L. Worthington (ed.) *Dimensions of Forgiveness: Psychological Research and Theological Perspectives*. Philadelphia: Templeton Foundation Press, 1998, 39ff.

11 In a 1991 study done by Margaret Poloma and George Gallup, Jr. assessing the implications of religious beliefs and practice on forgiveness, they found that while the vast majority (94%) of respondents said that it "was fairly, or even very important, for religious people to forgive, only 48% said that they usually tried to forgive others." Poloma, Margaret and George H. Gallup, Jr. "Forgiveness in the Population," cited in Worthington, *Dimensions of Forgiveness*. Also see Margaret M. Poloma and George Gallup, Jr., "Unless You Forgive Others: Forgiveness, Prayer, and Life Satisfaction" presented at

Society for the Scientific Study of Religion. Virginia Beach, VA. November, 1990.

[12] Rye, Mark S. and Kenneth I. Pargament, "Forgiveness and Romantic Relationships in College: Can It Heal a Wounded Heart?" *Journal of Clinical Psychology*, Vol. 58(4), 419-441 (2002). Also see Pargament, Kenneth I. and Mark S. Rye. "Forgiveness as a Method of Religious Coping" in *Dimensions of Forgiveness*, Worthington, (ed.), 59-78, 74.

About the Author

Rev. Dr. Cari Jackson has one passion that guides her life: to help people discover and live their authentic selves. Her ultimate goal is to bring healing to a broken world by using her gifts in preaching, teaching, counseling, and writing blended with her incredible heart of love. She believes that the world heals one person at a time.

Dr. Cari is the founder and director of Center of Spiritual Light, which provides interpersonal and interspiritual resources for individual and organizational healing, growth, empowerment, and transformation. She has also served as senior pastor at First Congregational Church of Stamford, interim senior pastor at First Presbyterian Church of Brooklyn, associate pastor at The Church St. Paul and St. Andrew (United Methodist), interim pastor and adjunct professor at Union Theological Seminary, and associate worship coordinator at The Riverside Church in New York City.

Prior to professional ministry, she had an extensive career in human resource administration, staff development, management training, organization development, and mediation in business and community organizations. Dr. Cari is the author of three other books: *The Gift to Listen, The Courage to Hear*; *For the Least of These*; and soon-to-be-released *For the Souls of Black Folks*.

Dr. Cari received her Doctor of Philosophy degree in Christian Social Ethics from Drew University, Master of Divinity from Union Theological Seminary, Juris Doctor from University of Maryland School of Law, and Bachelor of Arts in Psychology and Sociology from Oberlin College.

About Center of Spiritual Light

Informing, Reforming, Transforming

Founded in 2002, Center of Spiritual Light provides a range of holistic interspiritual resources for individuals, organizations, and communities to facilitate their ongoing transformation and growth. We do this by offering programs and services that help shed light on how to access and strengthen the essence of wholeness, freedom and power that is already within.

Programs and services:

- ❑ Counseling
- ❑ Executive Leadership Coaching
- ❑ Organizational Consulting
- ❑ Workshops, Retreats, and Webinars

For more information, contact:

Center of Spiritual Light
Address:　930 Grand Concourse #9D, Bronx, NY 10451
Phone:　347-597-8028
Website:　http://CenterOfSpiritualLight.org

CPSIA information can be obtained at www.ICGtesting.com
Printed in the USA
BVOW070805010513

319563BV00003B/467/P